The MONEY Basics

The MONEY Basics

HOW TO BECOME YOUR OWN FINANCIAL HERO

PETER KOMOLAFE

HarperCollins*Publishers*

HarperCollins*Publishers*
1 London Bridge Street
London SE1 9GF

www.harpercollins.co.uk

HarperCollins*Publishers*
Macken House, 39/40 Mayor Street Upper
Dublin 1, D01 C9W8, Ireland

First published by HarperCollins*Publishers* 2023

1 3 5 7 9 10 8 6 4 2

A catalogue record of this book is
available from the British Library

ISBN 978-0-00-862035-6

Printed and bound in the UK using 100%
renewable electricity at CPI Group (UK) Ltd

This book is dedicated to you, the reader. Your success in life is my mission. My hope is that your journey with money will be smooth and prosperous.

CONTENTS

HOW TO USE THIS BOOK AND KEY TERMS

The language of personal finance has always been full of jargon and technical terms, making some things that should be simple difficult to understand. You can read the book from cover to cover or select a section you want to study in more depth.

If you're looking for an easy way to get your bearings in personal finance, the following list of terms will help familiarise you with some basic concepts and terminology related to money and investments covered in this book.

If you're going to take control of your financial future and become your own financial hero, you need to understand the language used in finance. It will initially seem alien, but I promise as you grow in confidence it will become part of your vocabulary. The terms below are used every day by professional investors and ordinary people like you. Feel free to refer back to them as you please.

Appreciation

Appreciation is an increase in the value of an asset, like a home. Appreciation can be measured by comparing the current market value of the asset to its original cost. For example, if you bought a house for £200,000 and it's now worth £400,000 after five years, it's clearly appreciated in value.

APR

APR stands for annual percentage rate, which determines how much interest will be paid on a credit facility like a credit card. It's the official rate used to help you understand the cost of borrowing. It includes any fees or additional costs incurred to set up the facility.

Asset

An asset is anything your own that has value and can increase (appreciate) in value over time. An asset could include property, jewellery, artwork, investments or precious metals such as gold, silver and platinum.

Balance transfer

A balance transfer is a type of credit card transaction that moves a balance from one credit card to another. Typically, the balance being transferred is held on a credit card from a different credit card issuer with an introductory period when the balance transfer attracts no interest for an agreed time.

Bankruptcy

Bankruptcy is a legal proceeding initiated when a person or business cannot repay outstanding debts or obligations.

Central bank

A central bank is a bank that controls the money supply in a country. It usually sets interest rates and decides how much money to print. The Bank of England, Federal Reserve and European Central Bank are examples of central banks in the United Kingdom, United States and Europe, respectively.

Collateral

Something pledged as security for repayment of a loan, which can and will be forfeited in the event of a default.

Compound interest

Compound interest is when the interest you earn on your money earns interest on itself. For example, you deposit £100 into an account, and one year later, your £100 is now £110. In year two, you will earn interest on £110 instead of your original £100.

Consolidation

Consolidation is a way of merging your existing debts into one convenient monthly payment. This can be a good option when you have multiple debts (for example, on credit cards or overdrafts) that you wish to pay off within a more defined timeframe.

Credit report

Your credit report is a digital record of your financial history. It contains records of all your debts, your payment history, including missed and late payments, county court judgments and other court records registered against you. The information in your report is used to derive your credit score.

Credit score

A credit score is a number that shows the likelihood that you will pay back the money you borrow. Lenders use credit scores to determine whether to accept your application for credit facilities such as personal loans, mortgages or car loans. They also use your score to determine what interest rate to offer you.

Cryptocurrency (crypto)

A cryptocurrency is a digital or virtual currency that uses cryptography to secure its transactions. A cryptocurrency is difficult to counterfeit because of this security feature. Cryptocurrencies are not legal tender. No government or central bank currently backs them. Cryptocurrencies can be used to buy goods and services privately using peer-to-peer transactions, but they have to be exchanged for physical money first if you want to use them in the real world.

Debt

Debt is a loan of money that carries an obligation of repayment. It is a liability.

Debt prioritisation

Debt prioritisation is a way to decide which debts to pay first when you have multiple debts.

Debt relief orders

Debt relief orders (DROs) are a way of legally avoiding bankruptcy. They're designed for people with debts of less than £20,000 who can't afford to pay them back. A DRO lasts for three years; during that time, your creditors can't continue taking court action against you because they won't be able to get payment. If someone applies for a DRO and doesn't have enough money to repay their debts in full, they will have to make monthly payments once the order is granted – these payments are set at an affordable level for the person applying for it.

Depreciation

Depreciation is when an asset falls in value.

Forex

Forex stands for foreign exchange, which refers to the foreign exchange market, a global marketplace for trading one nation's currency for another – for example, trading the British pound for the US dollar or the euro.

FTSE 100

This is an index that tracks the performance of the 100 largest companies on the London Stock Exchange. The FTSE 100 is a good indicator of how the UK economy is doing and can be used as a benchmark for measuring the health of UK businesses.

Individual voluntary arrangements

An individual voluntary arrangement (IVA) is a formal debt-management plan that allows you to take control of your finances by paying back at least 50 per cent of your debts over an extended period. IVAs could be an option for people who want to avoid bankruptcy but need help managing their debt. They're available in England and Wales only.

Inflation

The rate at which prices for goods and services rise is called inflation. If inflation is high, money isn't worth as much as it once was. Inflation can be measured in various ways, including year-over-year comparisons, month-over-month comparisons, and even using specific categories like food or gas prices. Inflation also refers to a general increase in prices for goods and services over time. This occurs when supply does not meet demand – when there isn't enough money circulating within an economy to pay workers who need to buy food or rent homes with their wages – or when people have more money than they want to spend (excess savings).

Interest rates

An interest rate is the amount of money charged for borrowing money. Interest rates are usually expressed as a percentage of the amount borrowed. They are paid on all credit facilities like personal loans, car finance, credit cards, overdrafts, store cards, payday loans and mortgages. Interest can also be paid on a savings account by a bank or building society in exchange for you depositing money with them.

Investment

Investment is the act of purchasing an asset with the expectation of obtaining an additional income or profit.

Liability

A liability is anything you owe. It's usually considered a negative because it represents something you borrowed money for, and that debt must eventually be repaid with interest. Examples of liabilities include:

- credit cards
- student loans
- mortgages
- car finance
- payday loans
- store cards
- personal loans
- overdrafts.

Mortgage

A mortgage is a loan taken out to buy a home. If you are buying a house using a mortgage, the lender will take an interest in the property until you have paid off your mortgage in full. If you don't make these payments, your lender could take possession of your house or sell it at auction.

Net worth

Net worth is the difference between your assets and liabilities. It's a measure of wealth and financial security and can also measure your financial health.

Payday loans

A payday loan is a short-term loan that typically lasts for only a few weeks and is repaid when the borrower receives his or her next pay cheque. Payday loans are typically very expensive, with higher interest rates due to their short-term nature.

S&P 500

Standard & Poor's 500 (S&P 500) is an index based on the market capitalisations of 500 large companies with common stock listed on the New York Stock Exchange. The S&P 500 was created by Standard & Poor's, a division of McGraw Hill Financial.

Stock market

A stock market is a marketplace where you can purchase shares in publicly traded companies like Apple, Tesla, Amazon and Microsoft, to name a few.

Stock, shares, equities

These words are used interchangeably but essentially refer to the same thing. A share, stock or equity is a company like Apple, Tesla or Amazon publicly traded on a stock market.

INTRODUCTION

Welcome to the start of a new way of thinking about one of the most, if not the most, essential commodity in modern history and our lives: *money*. There are so many great quotes about money. Here are a few:

> **'Beware of small expenses; a small
> leak will sink a great ship.'**
> Benjamin Franklin

> **'You can be young without money,
> but you can't be old without it.'**
> Tennessee Williams

> **'Too many people spend money they haven't
> earned, to buy things they don't want, to impress
> people they don't like.'**
> Will Rogers

**'Money is like a sixth sense – and you can't
make use of the other five without it.'**

W. Somerset Maugham

These are some of my favourite quotes about money. They resonate with me because I can see the wisdom in these words, having struggled with money for most of my life.

The trouble with quotes like these is that we can easily forget them; they all sound like common sense, but if you have no practical way of applying them, they are little more than platitudes.

This book will help you to be better with money and will move you forward in a way that will benefit you for years to come. It will teach you to develop a set of habits that are transferable and repeatable. It will also help you build and maintain a healthy relationship with money to create the life you want. The book will give you the skills and knowledge you need to make sound financial decisions.

Bold claims, I know, but there is a catch. There is work for you to do. The B.A.S.I.C. formula I have devised for this book will form the basis for creating the life you aspire to have when it comes to money. Throughout its pages, you will find helpful exercises to help you assess where you are. You will document and set your goals, and gain a structure to create a better relationship with money.

I encourage you to complete the exercises. We will refer back to them throughout the book, and you will be in a much healthier place by the end.

WHO I AM

I was born in Dulwich Hospital on 22 November 1979, to Nigerian parents who came to the United Kingdom with dreams of building a better future. They named me Peter Oluwafemi Komolafe. Like many Nigerians who came to the United Kingdom back then, my parents worked multiple jobs and studied simultaneously. With three older boys to support, multiple jobs to hold down and the pressures of studying, they put me into foster care at three months old. Back then, it was customary for West African children and babies to be fostered via newspaper ads and childcare journals. So much for child safeguarding, but as crazy as that sounds, at three months old, they put me in the care of Sid and Sylvia Saunders, a young couple from Hastings, East Sussex, whom I fondly remember being a pivotal part of my early childhood.

In 1988, when I was eight, my parents, who had returned to Nigeria some years earlier, sent for me. What should have been a two-week holiday to meet my older brothers turned into a ten-year stay that saw me complete my primary and secondary education in Nigeria.

It was a strange period in my life. I met my family for the first time. I travelled beyond the shores of the UK for the first time, which was a culture shock. It was the first time I noticed a little thing called money. Money was the root cause of arguments, stress and, in many instances, desperation in our household. I recall hundreds, if not thousands, of arguments over money; what money had been spent, why it was spent, how it had been spent and how it never seemed that a naira (pound) or a kobo (penny) went far enough. Through those ten years, I developed an appreciation for many things we take for granted in the Western world: running water, steady electricity, three square meals and, most importantly, opportunity.

In October 1998, my parents mustered enough money to purchase a plane ticket back to the UK. With the plane ticket, they also found £50 to give me a head start. I remember waving goodbye to Mum and my brother at Murtala Muhammed International Airport, Lagos, filled with excitement and a strange sense of calm. I was venturing into the world on my own. My parents did their best to prepare me, and for much of my teenage years, they made no secret of the privilege I had been born with being a UK citizen. It was the luck of the draw, and compared with my three older brothers, I had a lottery ticket. My older brothers weren't that fortunate. I understood it, and I recognised it came with a responsibility to make the most of the opportunities that would come my way through no merit of my own. Since I was eight years old, I knew that a day of reckoning would come, and I had been dreaming about it. I was eighteen, five feet two inches tall, looked thirteen years old and had the maturity of a similar age. There was only one plan: head back to Quebec Road, Hastings, hoping that my long-estranged foster parents still lived there.

I couldn't sleep on the plane crossing, and the closer I got to touchdown, the more the reality of the situation dawned on me. What if I get sent back when I landed? I looked thirteen. What would I do if my foster parents, who hadn't heard from me in over a decade, didn't live on Quebec Road any more? What would I do if they didn't want to take me in? Who could I turn to? Where would I go? What would I do? The more those thoughts bubbled to the forefront of my mind, the more scared I became and, strangely, the calmer I felt. The dice had been rolled. Whatever happened, I was in it alone, and I had to become a man.

When the plane landed and I approached customs, I remember my heart beating out of my chest; I was nervous and terrified of being sent back the way I came. I remember the customs agent looking at my passport multiple times and then at me.

'Who's meeting you?' he asked.

'No one,' I replied.

'So, where are you going, and who are you staying with?'

I said I was heading to my foster parents in Hastings. I would stay with them.

After a few more minutes and a few more questions, he waved me through. I felt relief. The train journey to Hastings was a blur, but I remember getting off the train at Hastings train station and jumping into a taxi to Quebec Road. It was around 11.30 a.m. The sights were familiar, and it felt like home.

I pulled up to Quebec Road and knocked on the door expecting a familiar face, but the door didn't open. No one was home. In that moment, panic set in. Sure, I'd thought about this on the plane, but I hadn't really considered it. It was a weekday coming up to lunchtime. People were at work, but that didn't occur to me. I naturally thought the worst. Perhaps they had moved. Perhaps I was on a stranger's doorstep. All I could do was wait. It was at this point that I realised the difference in the climate. The temperature in Nigeria in October is between twenty-eight and thirty degrees. Here I was, in unsuitable clothing, trying to adjust to the fifteen-degree conditions with a single suitcase outside a house I wasn't sure my foster parents still lived in.

The wait felt like an eternity, but after a few hours a neighbour from across the road recognised me and sheltered me until my foster parents finished work. Luckily, they still lived at the same address after all this time, and, despite my arrival being a shock, they took me in and helped me find my feet.

My first few years back in the UK were troublesome. I had to readjust to the culture, the climate and the people. Social interactions were unpleasant because I looked thirteen. I became a victim of bullying. People took advantage of me, assaulted me and called me names, and through all this I realised I didn't know how to stand up for myself. I was a passive observer, a passenger on a journey I had no control over. I felt lost, clueless and utterly ill-prepared for the reality it thrust me into. It was my path to walk, but I did not know what the next steps were, and this not knowing ultimately led me to be homeless, sleeping rough on the cold streets of Hastings with nowhere to turn and no one to ask for help. Talk about becoming a man. Nothing prepares you and teaches you more powerfully about the harsh reality of life than being desolate.

Being homeless was tough. People automatically think you're the architect of your own downfall, which wasn't the case for me. Sure, I got on a plane without a plan. Some might say I was stupid and naïve, but I had dreams and hopes of a better life compared with the bush I'd stared out at every day in Nigeria. And strangely, despite my predicament, I was happy to be back where I knew I had access to opportunity. No matter how hard things got, I knew things could only improve.

I believe wholeheartedly that we are products of our experiences. Our lives are a mosaic of moments that amalgamate to create a beautiful picture. We realise our goals and purpose through epiphanies and other moments of clarity. I found what gives me my sense of purpose and fulfilment in an industry I fell into reluctantly. An industry that, against all odds, has afforded me opportunities and access to knowledge that every child in our education system should have access to. I went from sleeping on the streets to becoming part of an executive team of a Fortune 100 company in Canary Wharf (without a university degree). From there on I have had appearances on national television, and now I am writing this book. I've learnt that costly personal experiences carry lessons, lessons you don't have to learn the hard way.

WHAT I DO

As indicated above, I fell into the financial services industry by mistake and with a lot of reluctance. It was 2006; I was broke, on benefits and owed several banks money. Back then, I used to rack up bank charges like I was being rewarded for doing so. My credit score was on the floor. I was financially illiterate and incapable of making smart financial decisions. Life was about survival, and when you're in survival mode, you lose the ability to reason and make rational decisions. When you're in survival mode, it clouds your thought process with the necessity of covering the essentials. In my case, it led me into a financial spiral. I borrowed money to cover what I thought were basics, only to borrow more to pay off the previous debt, so the cycle continued. Simply put, I was terrible with money.

Back in 2006, working in financial services was prestigious. Financial services offered relatively well-paid jobs and excellent career progression prospects. I was forced to attend my first and only interview with a bank. It was an attractive proposition, but I knew I owed money to many banks, and one look at my credit score would immediately make me an unfit candidate. Besides, all previous communication I had with banks related to charge notifications. I thought it was a waste of time, but if I didn't go, I would lose my benefits, and I didn't want that to happen.

Looking back now, attending that interview was one of the pivotal moments of my career. It set into motion the wheels that made everything else that happened possible. It was also the first time I met someone who saw something in me I couldn't see myself.

Her name was Jenny Berry, and I'm sure that she'll be reading this, so thank you for giving a kid on his knees a chance all those years ago. She is why I find myself writing this book and ended up on the executive team of a Fortune 100 company. She is also the reason I have appeared in the media and on shows like *Steph's Packed Lunch* and *Secret Spenders* (Channel 4), *Lorraine* (ITV), GB News, the *Sun*, BBC World Service, the *Metro*, *The Times*, the *Express*, the *Daily Mail*, *Morning Brew*, BBC Radio, the *Voice* newspaper, BBC Sound Advice and so many more.

I am passionate, driven and obsessed about sharing the knowledge I've gained through sixteen years of working in financial services with ordinary people in a meaningful, relatable way. Through my podcast and my YouTube channel, I use my experiences and lessons learnt to help people understand the important financial principles that underlie financial success. It isn't rocket science, but it is logical and systematic. My job is to help you understand the logic and get to grips with the systems and habits that will help you become your own financial hero.

For far too long we have shrouded subjects such as investing in misconceptions, misinformation and untruths. You come across these untruths every day; investing is only for the wealthy, investing is too risky, you need sizeable sums of money to invest ... I could go on. The financial services industry has spent decades perpetuating these untruths for its own gain. They have ransacked the hopes and dreams of the less fortunate under the façade that you need them because it's all too complicated. They have made billions of pounds, paid their executives hundreds of millions in remuneration and caused global recessions. We have bailed them out, and through all of this they have become unaccountable for their actions. They are not alone in bearing the blame. Our governments have aided them through a lack of effective regulation, deregulation and a total disregard for real financial education in our school system. Instead, the banks play the role of educator to our children, whose earliest interaction with them is often when opening their first account. We then introduce kids to financial products such as overdrafts and credit cards, and we trust the banks to have an unbiased conversation, disregarding their bottom line.

My career in financial services has taken me through retail banking, corporate banking and wealth management. For most of my career, I have worked in positions where I have seen first-hand what money means to ordinary people who work hard for what they have and aspire to a decent quality of life. Be it as a financial adviser or consultant working with financial advisers, I have come to realise how little we know about money through no fault of our own. And throughout those years, I couldn't help but feel a sense of despair in knowing what I know but realising that ordinary people don't know it. I kept thinking to myself, I wish I had known this when I was twenty-two or twenty-three. Why didn't anyone talk to me about this when I was that age? It would have made a massive difference. I wouldn't have spent fifteen years in debt, and certainly would have made better financial decisions and cultivated healthy financial habits sooner.

What I do for a living differs from that of the popular names you might hear and think of in personal finance. I am not Martin Lewis. As great as Martin is, there is more to your financial life than saving money in the highest-yielding savings account you can find. Yes, it's an essential element to your financial stability, but it's only a tiny part of a larger, more beautiful tapestry of skills and habits you need to knit together.

My ambition isn't just to help people save money. It's to help you understand what to do with the money you earn and how to safely build for the future without the hyperbole commonly associated with investing nowadays. My mission is to help you become your own financial hero. Let's get started!

BECOMING YOUR OWN FINANCIAL HERO

In the early 2000s, I was broke and on benefits. I was in a lot of debt, and in a pretty terrible place. I was on my way out of a hostel that served as a transition from sleeping rough on the streets. Despite being relieved to have the council provide me with a place to live, I was filled with apprehension about the future. My confidence was non-existent back then, and I felt alone. A hero was what I needed.

Hero (noun): A person noted for courageous acts or nobility of character.

Synonyms associated with the word 'hero' include champion, victor, winner, conqueror, star, idol, lionheart and warrior.

In life, we all have our heroes, people we look up to, champions we admire, warriors who have overcome overwhelming odds to achieve something great and are a beacon of what is possible for all of us. These heroes can be family members, friends, or maybe even celebrities. If I asked you who your hero is, the person you choose would most likely fall into one of those groups. Sometimes we have more than one hero, and they might change as we evolve and grow through life.

Some of my early heroes who I looked up to were the rappers of the 1990s. They helped me stay positive and dream beyond the bush I was seeing from my window in Nigeria. As I've grown and developed, my heroes have changed. One of my most important of recent time has been Barack Obama. I admire his poise, and the tenacity it takes to be a notable public figure, with all the scrutiny that attracts, and still hold yourself with dignity. For me, he is an example of what is possible against all the odds and a testament to how time changes all things.

But why am I talking about heroes and what relevance do they have? There is a lot we can learn and mirror from our heroes in our personal endeavours. Sometimes we need to see an example of what we aspire to be so we can learn, replicate and adapt our approach towards the same thing. We might see a character trait, notice a moment, an act, or hear a word that gives us the kick we all need. Sometimes, the smallest things can catalyse the biggest changes in our lives.

For the longest time, I didn't realise I had what it took to be my own financial hero. Too often we look to others to be the catalyst for the change, when we already have what's required. Ironically, the thing that stops us is courage. I couldn't muster the courage to face my debt problems head-on and that's how most of us feel about the situations we face, especially when it comes to money. We feel ill-equipped and ashamed of where we find ourselves, despite our never having been given the tools to make better decisions all along. Most of us interact with financial products at the point where we have a pressing need. In my experience, that's the worse time for decision making, as our decisions can be irrational, driven by need instead of logic.

In moments like these, and there are many of them, we need to be our own financial hero. In such moments, our heroes can't swoop in and save us, no inspirational quote can give us the answers we need. Instead, we make a decision that we hope is the right one.

WHAT DOES BECOMING YOUR OWN FINANCIAL HERO MEAN?

I'm writing this book amid the 2022 cost-of-living crisis, where we have seen energy prices rise by over 200 per cent, interest rates reach heights we haven't seen in decades, and inflation in double digits for the first time since the 1970s. Millions of households across the country are feeling the pinch, and every week on Channel 4 I hear stories of real people struggling to survive. Many feel a sense of helplessness as the financial pressure builds.

Naturally, in a crisis such as this, people are affected differently. At one end of the spectrum, you have those who are impacted the most. They see a significant impact on their standard of living and find themselves worse off, with access to little to no help. In the middle are those who are moderately affected, but they can adjust and maintain the same standard of living. At the far end, you have those with abundant resources who barely feel it. Those are the 1 per cent.

Becoming your own financial hero doesn't mean being in the 1 per cent. It simply means being in a position where you can change to weather whatever storm you face. Becoming your own financial hero is about having the courage to face your financial challenges and having the character to be open and vocal about your relationship with money. Being a champion in your pursuit of financial security is what it is about. It concerns having the financial habits and a skill-set that allow you to create your life and how you aspire to live it. It will make you less reliant on others and less constrained by the norms of a nine-to-five job. You will gain a sense of autonomy and independence, with the ability to make choices out of a sense of freedom, not necessity.

Let me use an analogy. Imagine playing chess as a complete novice against a grandmaster. Not only is the game a mismatch, but you're also not equipped to win. Unfortunately, with financial matters, most of us are ill-equipped.

Becoming your own financial hero is about taking charge and putting the ball in your court. How many times have you felt helpless and had a lack of control over your financial life? As your own financial hero, those feelings of stress, anxiety and helplessness will be a thing of the past. As your own financial hero, you will feel empowered, financially capable, confident and secure in your financial life.

HOW DO YOU BECOME YOUR OWN FINANCIAL HERO?

I can speak from personal experience when I tell you there isn't a quick fix or cheat code to achieving this. Like most things in life, it demands effort and dedication.

If I look back over my journey, it's been full of trial and error, and I've had to learn from my mistakes. Unfortunately, I didn't have anyone to help me navigate key decisions. I didn't have a family member I could ask or a trusted person to pass on things they had learnt, and I think that's the same for most people as they grow up learning about money. We all muddle our way through, hoping for the best, and later realise that we missed something important because we didn't know the right questions to ask. What makes this worse is the idea that we should know better and that the onus is on us to make the best decision. Throughout my time in Canary Wharf, a saying resonated with me and speaks volumes about what we think we know. I'm not sure if it's a popular saying, but it goes: *'You don't know what you don't know till you know you don't know it.'*

This statement applies to most things in life, but it's particularly pertinent to this conversation about money. In Canary Wharf, I learnt so much about matters I didn't even know existed. For example, I did not know what dividend investing was. I didn't even know you could buy shares in a company like Apple, let alone receive part of their profits. The first time I found out about this, I was like ... what? It's impossible to know the right question to ask if you don't have access to all the information or aren't aware of the right information to seek. The financial services industry has never been concerned with educating its customers. They give you just about enough information to nudge you to a decision, but make no mistake, if the decision you make turns out to be the wrong one, you're the adult. It was your responsibility.

To become your own financial hero, you must be eager to learn, to ask the right questions in order to make the right decisions. It will require hard work, a conscious effort and discipline, but the rewards are worth it. Imagine being in a position where you have no debts and no real financial pressure, and you get to live your life doing something you enjoy and being paid for it. This is the dream that social media sells to you every day, and at the heart of this dream is your ability to make money. What they leave out is what to do with said money, and that's where I come in.

I am lucky enough to be in the position I just described. I have no debts and no financial pressures, and I spend my days being paid to do something I love. It's a galaxy away from where I was in the early 2000s, and you, too, can make it to a similar place. Together, you and I are going to take the first step. Right now.

THE B.A.S.I.C. FORMULA

The B.A.S.I.C. formula is my take on the five financial habits you need to develop in order to become your own financial hero. These are habits I learnt to develop through trial and error; lessons from working in the financial services. I learnt them from observing wealthy clients I have advised and influential people I have interacted with.

Nothing in this formula is new or revolutionary, but it is a very simple, easy-to-grasp concept that will help you make better financial decisions and give you control over your finances. If you take nothing else from this book, remember the following five principles: B – Budget, A – Avoid Debt, S – Save Early, I – Invest Early, C – Credit Score.

We will delve into each of these principles individually, with practical tips to help you. Each of the principles relies on the others to work. Together, they are the building blocks upon which you will begin to build your financial security and future wealth. Each principle relies on the one before it for stability and ultimate success, so please pay close attention to every one.

This formula has transformed my finances and it has freed me from the shackles of a high-paying nine-to-five job and enabled me to pursue my dreams and create financial security. It has allowed me to lay the path to this moment, writing this book for you. It has changed my life and I am confident it will change yours too.

YOUR WHY AND TIME

'Setting goals is the first step in turning the invisible into the visible.'
Tony Robbins

Let me tell you something you probably already know, and if you don't, you need to know: when you can't think one year ahead, you won't be able to think five or ten years ahead, and before you know it, you've gone nowhere.

When I was fifteen and in Nigeria, I saw my dad panicking about something called a pension. I didn't know then what a pension was, but it clearly had Dad – who by then was well into his fifties – scared. My dad was never scared. He was the most remarkable, hard-working person I knew. A few years after he turned fifty, he returned to school to gain another master's degree, simply because he wanted to. Despite how highly studious my dad was, he wasn't savvy about money. He hadn't planned for his retirement and found himself approaching it with no provisions. He didn't own his own home and realised he would never be financially secure. In the end, my dad died working well into his late sixties. He came home one day feeling run-down with a headache and never woke up.

I am sharing this story because I want you to ask yourself the fundamental questions I believe drive us all. Why are you here? Why do you go to work? What do you want from life?

Do you want to spend each day under constant financial pressure, or do you want to live with a sense of financial security and freedom?

Many of us have goals for everything but our finances. Think about it. You probably have a fitness goal if you're into fitness. You have a business goal if you run your own business or are an entrepreneur. If you work within a business as an employee, you have career goals. So, why don't we have financial goals?

Here's the definition of what financial goals are.

> Financial goals are targets an individual sets to achieve financial milestones or plans. They are financial objectives that an individual wishes to accomplish within a certain time frame.

Here's another definition of what financial goals are.

> Financial goals are the personal, big-picture objectives you set for how you'll save and spend money. They can be things you hope to achieve in the short term or further down the road.

There will be a monetary requirement for most things you want to do in life. If you want to get on the property ladder, you need money. You want to send your kids to university? You need money. You want more flexibility to work less and spend more time on things you enjoy, or with your family? You need money. You want to retire early? You need money. Very few things in our lives are not connected to money and our ability to deploy it effectively. Setting a financial goal is a more targeted and focused way of approaching your life goals while at the same time proactively tackling the financial element.

For example, your goal might be getting onto the property ladder. This is a life goal and a financial goal. Financially, the question becomes: how much is this going to cost? What property price range are you shopping in? What level of deposit do you need? And how are you going to acquire said deposit? In this instance, your financial goal is your deposit, which will be a specific amount of money that you need to raise.

TASK 1

This is the first exercise we are embarking on together. It will take about thirty minutes, but it will be a worthwhile thirty minutes by the time we get to the end. The exercise aims to help you step back and take a high-level snapshot of where you are right now, but more importantly, of the goals and aspirations that will move you forward to the place you want to be. This could be a year or four years into the future. You will need to take note and score yourself in specific areas of your life, and once that's done, we will delve into the financial aspect of your life to set some goals to work towards.

For best results, you need a pen, a pad and a quiet space where you won't be disturbed. If you haven't got a quiet place or are on the move, note your thoughts later. The most important ingredient for success with this exercise is your ability to be honest with yourself. The scores you record are not an indictment of you or anything you've done before. Only you will know the scores you end up with, so there's no pressure.

Part 1: The Wheel of Life

Paul J. Meyer, who founded the Success Motivation® Institute in 1960, created the wheel of life. This tool has been widely used to help people find balance and focus. All the areas it explores are meaningful to us as individuals, some more so than others. When exploring each of them, we can prioritise what matters the most and pour our energy into those that give us a sense of purpose and fulfilment.

Here's what I want you to do. Take ten minutes to score yourself between 1 and 10 in each of the slices you see in the circle. Your task isn't to score ten in each area. This is where honesty comes in. Be truthful, don't front, and don't allow bravado or a sense of pride to influence your score. You'd only be cheating yourself.

Now that you've scored yourself, how have you done? In what areas did you score well? In what areas not so well? And in which did you score mid-range? Time for more honesty. Ask yourself why you scored yourself as you did. Note those answers down. Again, please don't front, don't sugar-coat it for yourself. Receive it as an honest self-assessment of those areas of your life.

There will be some areas you care more about than others. For instance, at this precise moment, my scores across all the areas would vary from high to mid to low.

I would score myself an 8 for finances, 6 on health, 3 on friends and family, 8 on romance, 7 on personal growth, 3 on fun and recreation, 7 on physical environment and a 6 on business and career.

There are many reasons for my scores. I am focused on my business and my career, but there is so much more to be done. The 6 I scored represents the progress I would like to make and some things that aren't ready within my business yet. I have few friends, and the friends I have I rarely see because we live in different parts of the country, and so family and business get in the way. I want to improve this as I feel I've lost touch with some of them. A 3, then, is a fair reflection of what I feel concerning friends and family. Financially, I feel as stable as I have ever been, and I will share more on this as we progress through the book.

Look at how you've scored, and you will see areas where you may want to focus. A significant area of improvement for me would be friends, which may mean making more of a conscious effort for online meets or speaking more regularly to reconnect. Another area would be fun and recreation, taking more time off from the business to travel and explore the world.

Those are examples of the areas on which I will focus. What are your key areas, and what will you do to improve them? Write them down and prioritise them in the order of what's most important to you.

Part 2: The Finance Wheel

We're now going to take this exercise one step further and focus on your finances. Much like before, please be honest about your score. You will see better results in the short to long term if you are honest and transparent with yourself.

Take ten minutes to score yourself between 1 and 10 in each of the slices you see in the circle. The question you need to ask yourself when scoring here is how happy or confident are you in each of these areas. Are you satisfied with the way you budget? With the level of savings you have? Is your retirement preparation going well? Are you paying into a pension for retirement? Do you invest for your future, and if so, are you satisfied with your investments? Do you have a good credit score? And finally, how do you feel about the debt you have? Do you have debt?

Here's how I would score myself.

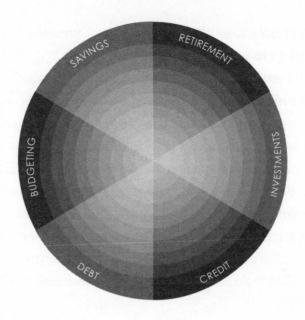

Budgeting, 9
Savings, 8
Retirement, 7
Investments, 6
Credit, 9
and Debt, 9

Here are my reasons for the scores I have given myself. My budget is tight. I review it often, and I have a really good set-up that works for me. I gave myself an 8 for savings because I have a pretty good safety net to keep me afloat at any given time. I could have scored higher, but at the moment I hold too much in my savings. I'm a 7 for retirement because I have existing retirement investments, but I've slowed down how much I'm paying into my retirement fund while growing my business. We could say the same for the reason behind my score for investments. I'm reinvesting back into my business. I gave myself a 9 on credit because I have a very high score and an immaculate credit report. We will talk about this more in later chapters. Finally, I scored myself a 9 on debt because I have no debt apart from a small mortgage. More on this later.

Over to you. How did you score? Are there any surprises? How do you feel about the scores you've ended the exercise with? What are the main areas that jumped out at you, and what areas do you want to improve? Write them down in order of importance, and add the emotion you're feeling next to each one. For example, I used to be in debt. The emotions that I most commonly felt were shame and anxiety. Be honest about how you feel and note it down.

That's the hard bit. Now, in the third and final part of the exercise, we're going to move on to looking towards your future goals and aspirations.

Part 3: Your Timeline

You will need ten minutes for this part of the exercise. Ask yourself, where would you want to see yourself if you could jump into a DeLorean and travel twenty years, thirty years into the future? Where would you be? What kind of life are you living then? Are you happy? Are you content?

As a financial planner, I used this exercise to help my clients visualise their future goals, aspirations and priorities. I use this with coaching clients to this day. Here's how it works. Pick four areas of your life that are of importance to you. You may choose to pick areas from your wheel of life that you've scored low on that are now a priority, or you might choose others – career,

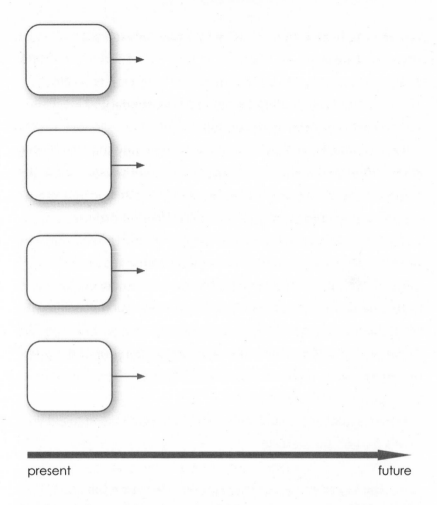

present   future

health, debt and family. It could be any variation of the areas from earlier. You could be specific and write a goal towards which you want to work. This could include objectives like home owner-ship, clearing debt, saving for a holiday to the Maldives or starting a business.

Once you decide what your four areas are, I want you to think about where you are and a point in the future. That point in the future could be three, five or even twenty years from now. Once you note down that point, I want you to visualise and write what

33

you want to have achieved and why the achievement matters to you. I also want you to record how you would feel if you didn't achieve your goals and what that would mean in the future.

For example, what does a good retirement look and feel like, if you chose retirement on the timeline? How much income do you think you would need? Do you want to take a holiday each year and change your car every three years? Think about the practicalities of what life would be like and feel like. If you fail to achieve a good retirement, what will be the implications?

If your goal is to get onto the property ladder, what kind of property do you want to buy? How many bedrooms does it have? Does it have a garden? How big is the garden? Where do you want to purchase when it comes to location? How much does it cost? What deposit do you need? Visualise the property, walk through it, open the doors, open the windows, visualise the rooms furnished, what pictures you would have on the walls and so forth, and note how it all feels.

Here's a quote on visualisation I'd like you to take in to aid you in this part of the exercise.

'The key to effective visualisation is to create the most detailed, vivid and clear picture to focus on.'

Most of the milestones I've achieved professionally and personally have been a by-product of visualisation. I began to visualise working in Canary Wharf after walking around the area back in 2007 and picturing what it would be like to work there. My appearing on national television and featuring in numerous press articles all started with visualising what it would be like and how it would feel. If you can picture it in your mind's eye, you can make it happen and, for me, it subconsciously put me on track.

The only thing left to do is set clear goals that will put you on the path to achieving your goals in the four areas you've chosen, visualised and made notes on. We will refer to these goals throughout the rest of this book. When you set your goals, the following points are crucial for success.

1. It's great to think and dream big, but what we want to be is specific and establish the small steps to your goal. Back to the house example from earlier. The deposit you need is £X, but what are the steps to £X? How much can you afford to save towards your deposit of £X, and how long do you have to save for it? Answering these questions will help you set the actual goals for which you will be accountable.

2. An unrealistic goal isn't a goal. It's a dream. We live in the real world, so your target must be rooted in the real world and be in accordance with your capabilities. There is no point in setting a goal of buying a £1 million mansion if you're on a £30,000-a-year income. Instead, a more realistic goal might be centred upon increasing your income or creating a business that will one day position you to buy a £1 million house.

3. Hold yourself accountable. Being committed to achieving your goals and holding yourself accountable is crucial. Better yet, find someone, a family member, friend or colleague, to be your accountability buddy. This can help you stay motivated and keep you on track when you feel like giving up. I've had an accountability buddy for many years, and there's something about knowing you will be called

upon to report your progress that keeps you motivated. I used to have weekly accountability calls. You may choose a monthly call or whatever works for you. If you can't find an accountability buddy, make sure that you are tracking, yourself, the progress you make. If your goal is to save a deposit for your first home, you can use an Excel tracker or set up a separate account just for your deposit. Seeing and documenting the progress you're making towards your goals is as important as the first and second steps you take.

PART 1

B: BUDGETING

As I boarded the plane to return to the UK in 1998, I was put in charge for the first time of money that was mine. Prior to that moment, I wasn't allowed to have my own money. Any money I was gifted was taken from me and put towards the needs of the family and our household. Things were tight. Back then, we had no running water and only intermittent electricity. Sometimes we relied on our neighbours for our meals. What little money we had, had to last. Fifty pounds was a lot of money and when I arrived back in the UK on that first day, I was so excited that the first thing I did was buy my favourite chocolate bars that I hadn't had for ten years. I spent almost a fiver on Snickers, Twix and Mars bars.

You would think that it would have registered. I had to conserve as much of the £50 I had for as long as possible and not waste it on chocolate treats. I had no comprehension of what budgeting or managing money was. I had no one to teach me and no genuine appreciation for the trouble I would later encounter. Even a base-level understanding of budgeting would have saved me years of anxiety and stress if I had possessed that fundamental skill.

Let's talk about why budgeting is the foundation upon which you build anything and everything you aspire to create, how to budget with purpose, how to make the change sustainable and how to know it's working.

> **'Money habits are set by age seven.'**
> David Whitebread and Sue Bingham,
> University of Cambridge

Back in 2013, research from behavioural experts David Whitebread and Sue Bingham of the University of Cambridge found that our financial habits and our approach to money, such as planning ahead, are formed by age seven. It's astonishing when you think about it. Seven is a very tender age, but as children there is so much that we subconsciously absorb that I'm not surprised. The takeaway from this is that it's very hard to reverse the associated habits of instant gratification later in life. It's not impossible, but it isn't easy.

Knowing this has helped me make sense of my past experiences with budgeting and money, but there is another factor that significantly impacted my early views and habits with money. It's a question I asked myself about seven years ago, and it's one I want you to think about and document the answer to: *What is your first memory when it comes to money?*

Most people can't answer this without really thinking about it. It took me years to pinpoint two key memories I believe shaped how I viewed money and my inability to budget and manage it effectively.

I can pinpoint the first memory from when I was six or seven years old. I remember my best friend and neighbour having dinners that smelt heavenly. The aromas coming from his kitchen at dinner time were different to ours and I always wondered why.

I can pinpoint the second memory from when I was about nine years old. I was in Nigeria. I was attending school and noticed other children had nicer things than me. Back then, I was an anomaly in school. I looked like all the other children, but I spoke with an English accent and couldn't speak the native language. I was this special kid that stuck out for all the wrong reasons but wasn't cool for all the right ones. One day, I asked my parents if they were broke. They laughed at me.

It seems harmless, but I realise that a mindset of scarcity was embedded pretty early in my development: initially, when I was around six or seven, and again, when I was nine. This scarcity mindset was responsible for most of the financial mistakes I made when I started to earn decent money. It led me to spending money like the rappers I idolised as a teen. I'm talking about Puffy (Puff Daddy, Diddy), Ma$e, The Notorious B.I.G. – they were my role models. I looked up to them and, as a teen, they told me to throw my 'Rollie in the sky', to pop champagne. The Notorious B.I.G. had me hypnotised. Going into adulthood, their influence persisted, and it took a shift in mindset to break free from a false narrative about what it looks like to be successful. The phrase 'Champagne taste on an Aldi budget' comes to mind.

You cannot underestimate the influence that our idols or social media have on our decisions as adults. I bet if you questioned how you come to purchasing decisions, external factors have more of an influence than you might want to admit. Brands are built on our propensity to be influenced; they count on that influence outweighing our ability to rationalise our financial decisions.

TASK 2

Here's a quick task. Think about the last five purchases you made and ask yourself how you came to the decision to make those purchases. Which were driven by a genuine need? Which were impulsive buys? Were you influenced in any way and how were you influenced? Note down your answers.

> **'If you have a different mindset, you will have a different outcome.'**
>
> Jack Ma

The most effective way to develop and embed new habits or behaviours is through intrinsic motivations. In part 3 of Task 1, you were asked to document your goals and place them on a timeline. This is to give you a documented record of your goals and what's important to you.

Intrinsic and extrinsic motivations can be quite nuanced and are an interesting part of behavioural science. Intrinsic motivation requires no specific reward to perform a task or do a thing. Most people who are intrinsically motivated do something because they enjoy it. For example, you play a sport because you enjoy it. Extrinsic motivation requires a reward or recognition of some form. For example, you play sports because you can win a trophy.

This speaks directly to our mindsets when we approach something new and maybe even something uncomfortable, like money. There has to be an extrinsic motivation leading to a reward to prompt or elicit action, but in the long run you need intrinsic motivation to keep it going. That's why part 3 of Task 1 is so important. You need to identify your goals and why it's important to establish your intrinsic and extrinsic motivations. Your extrinsic motivation is what your goal is (the reward, the thing you will accomplish), your intrinsic motivation is the why behind the what. Please review what you noted in that exercise and reflect on it. We will come back to the points you noted there throughout this book.

CHAPTER 1

BUDGETING WITH PURPOSE

I know how boring and utterly soul-destroying the idea of budgeting can be. I used to feel the same. Budgeting used to have a massive negative connotation for me. It was boring and restrictive. Something poor people did because they were poor. A constant reminder of how badly my life had turned out and of my place on the socioeconomic ladder. If you want to become your own financial hero you must understand that budgeting is the foundation of everything.

Think of the Shard, an iconic architectural masterpiece majestically gracing the London skyline. The Shard took three years, £1.2 billion and the expertise of 1,450 workers from sixty countries to build it. As majestic as it is, the Shard has a crucial component that is fundamental to the building's existence. Can you guess what it is? The answer is simple: a strong foundation.

A firm foundation ensures that a building is safe, can withstand storms and, ultimately, the test of time. The same principles apply to your finances. You cannot become your own financial hero and create financial security without a solid foundation. This is the single most important principle we will cover in this book, and I cannot stress how important it is that you secure your foundations. Without it, you can write off all the goals you identified in part 3 of Task 1.

The biggest misconception most of us harbour is that budgeting has to be complicated. Your budget, in reality, could be a simple, straightforward plan jotted down on a scrap of paper. Here's all you need to do.

1. Grab a piece of paper and draw a line down the middle. On one side, write how much you have coming in each month. On the other, list all your monthly expenses. Add up those expenses and subtract the amount from your total income.
2. You're left with a number. Hopefully, that number puts you in the surplus after all your expenses are accounted for. If you're in the minus, there's further work you will need to do to bring yourself back into balance.

That's a very simple budget that can be effective, but as with most things, the devil is in the detail. The most successful people I know have a knack for detail, which works for them professionally and personally; applying it to your finances is a real game changer. Taking a more pragmatic approach to your budget will enable you to assign your money to the things that matter to you. To do this, you must think about a budget differently. Let me explain.

We all have the essentials we have to pay for and keep up. These will account for a portion of our monthly outgoings, and that proportion will depend on where you live and several other factors. For example, if you live in London, you will probably have a larger proportion of your income allocated to rent compared with if you lived in Sheffield or other areas of the United Kingdom. In an ideal world, all of your essential expenditures (rent or mortgage, council tax, gas, electricity, food, loans, car finance, credit cards etc.) should amount to a certain percentage of your monthly income with enough left over for other expenses, such as your non-essentials.

Your non-essentials will be things you're not contractually obliged to pay for and that are not essential requirements. Things like Netflix, Apple TV, Disney Plus, gym memberships, magazine subscriptions, eating out, holidays and other luxuries come under this umbrella. Added up these will amount to a certain percentage of your income.

Most people stop here when they budget, but one further step will ensure you are budgeting with purpose. This further step will allow you to work towards the goals you noted in part 3 of Task 1 earlier. To illustrate this extra step, see the table below.

ESSENTIALS	NON-ESSENTIALS	OTHER

There are lots of ways you can divide your income across these three pots when you're pulling together your budget. It isn't complicated, but I have noticed this as a theme with every successful or wealthy person I've worked with. The budget that works best with this formula is composed of three distinct pots. Your essentials, non-essentials and your 'other' pot. We'll spend some time considering each of the three pots and how this would work in practice, and we'll go over some practical tips you will find helpful.

CHAPTER 2

THE ESSENTIALS

In 2015, I was working in Canary Wharf. I had recently passed my financial adviser exams and worked with a financial adviser on a pension planning case. One thing a financial adviser does with a client is fact-find. A fact-find is a deep dive into a client's life, exploring everything from how healthy their finances are to their assets, their liabilities and their future aspirations. Think of it as the construction blueprints for the Shard. The fact-find also goes into a client's income and expenditure – a budget – and lays out what foundations they have in place for us to build upon.

The client in question, let's call him Doug, was relatively successful. He was a senior-level executive, and despite the stereotype that might spring to mind, he displayed no outward manifestation of his wealth or financial status. As a consultant working on the case, I was privy to Doug's income and expenditure. What I saw astounded me and not only sent me into a mental spiral but shattered any prior notions that rich people are fast and loose with their cash.

Despite Doug's high-income level, his expenditure compared with his income was low. You might assume the opposite –

high income, high outgoings – but you'd be wrong. Doug operated from a mindset that he wanted to keep and maximise as much of his earnings as possible. This meant treating every instance of spending his money as though it were a business decision, like a professional. For most of us, that may come across as a very impersonal or robotic way to approach your budget, but I would later realise there was a method to this madness.

> **'It's not how much money you make, but how much money you keep.'**
> Robert Kiyosaki

In *Rich Dad Poor Dad*, Robert Kiyosaki said the above. He goes on to add that it's also about how hard it works for you and how many generations you can keep it for. This is a mentality I found common among wealthy clients and it perfectly underpins how they approach budgeting. Doug was the same, and when I asked why he allocated his money the way he did, his answer was very simple. He said, 'I don't spend money on things that don't matter.'

We've already identified that your essentials are the things you must pay for. They are essential to survival. You can't live without them.

To recap, your essentials will include the following:

rent,
mortgage,
electricity,
gas,

council tax,

water,

food,

any debt repayments (including car finance payments, loan
payments, credit card payments, store cards, payday
loans, student loans),

mandatory insurances policies (car insurance, buildings
insurance), transportation or fuel costs, phone and
broadband connectivity costs.

In the early 2000s, I worked at one of the local H. Samuel
stores in Hastings, East Sussex. Until then, every job that I had
had paid monthly. So, I was accustomed to paying my bills
monthly. This job paid weekly, so every Friday I would get
paid, but in my head I hadn't registered that I also needed to
budget for my bills weekly. I'm sure you can see where this is
going. Come to the end of the month, and I didn't have my rent.
I'm embarrassed to share this story, but I do so because sometimes budgeting with purpose requires us to be proactive and
alert to what's happening in our lives and around us. This
includes adapting our budget to suit the circumstances. I failed
at this miserably.

In Doug's case, he was actively allocating 40 per cent of his
income to his essential bills. This number may be different for
you, and if you live in an expensive city like London, this part
of your budget could be up to 60 per cent of your income,
possibly more. Whatever proportion of your income it is, this is
your priority. If you get this wrong, you will end up as I did,
with no money to pay my rent or other essential bills and probably utilising debt to cover your shortfall.

This part of your budget is important for your overall wellbeing, particularly your mental health. Most people worried about money are most concerned about covering their essentials.

Recent studies have found that you are 4.6 times more likely to have depression and 4.1 times more likely to have anxiety if you are worried about money. Financial worries have skyrocketed in recent years. If you think back to the pandemic and to the subsequent cost-of-living crisis, most people have had to take a long, hard look at their finances and financial habits.

Much like the foundations of the Shard, this part of your budget is your foundation. It's essential, pun intended. The more you can lock this down, the better peace of mind you will experience and the more financially stable you will feel. There is a key consideration that I haven't mentioned, a trap I have fallen into, and most people fall into during their working life.

When I started making decent money in Canary Wharf, it was completely life changing. I was earning the money that was a dream just years ago. I had fantasised about Canary Wharf since I started in financial services. When I began my role there in 2012, I started on a £28,000 basic salary with commission to boot. I used to watch *The Apprentice* and remember the fly-over at Canary Wharf and the tall building with the pointy top. Somehow, I found myself in that same building on the fiftieth floor, fulfilling a dream I never thought would come true. It was my opportunity to get my head down and seize the opportunity in front of me. If I were ever going to earn enough money to buy a house and build some financial security, this would be the place. Fast-forward a few years and a couple of promotions, and I earned a lot of money. I remember one of my bonus payments coming in at £25,000. My brain was doing backflips, the number was incomprehensible, and it was the first time I felt as though I had made progress in my journey. Deep down, I was still that kid who got off the plane with £50 in my pocket, had been homeless and was terrible with money.

As most people do in this position, I made the mistake of lifestyle creeping. I bought a nicer car (with a bigger monthly payment), I started shopping at more upmarket places and buying more expensive things, and in the end my increased income came with increased expenses because I upgraded my lifestyle. I got ahead of myself. At one point, I had a car on finance that cost more than my monthly mortgage payment, which significantly pushed up my essentials, and in hindsight it was unnecessary. Let me be clear, I am not advocating depriving yourself of the nice things you enjoy, but think it through beforehand. This is where you will feel the most financial pressure. The tighter you can keep this, the more financially secure you are going to feel.

Key Points to Remember and Action

1. To recap, your essentials will include the following: rent, mortgage, electricity, gas, council tax, water, food, any debt repayments (including car finance payments, loan payments, credit card payments, store cards, payday loans, student loans), mandatory insurances policies (car insurance, buildings insurance), transportation or fuel costs, phone and broadband connectivity costs.

2. Most people worried about money are most anxious about covering their essentials. This is the most important part of your budget.

3. You need to think very carefully before adding to or increasing this part of your budget. This is where you will feel the most financial pressure or security.

4. Budgeting is important for your overall wellbeing, particularly your mental health. If you're worried about covering your essentials, you're probably going to be anxious and stressed.

5. Don't get ahead of yourself and fall prey to lifestyle creep.

CHAPTER 3

THE NON-ESSENTIALS

Doug allocated 25 per cent of his income each month to his non-essentials. It was one of the first times I noticed someone actively plan for expenses I previously never paid attention to. I think many people are like this. We have a myriad of things that have our full attention – family, work, business and others. Such matters take precedence and sometimes become part of our subconscious routine.

Your non-essential expenses are the accoutrements that make the rigours of what you do for your money worthwhile. They will be things that aren't essential to your existence. We must acknowledge these and box them away mentally as negotiables if we ever run into financial difficulties.

However, it's also important to acknowledge the role of non-essential expenses in our day-to-day lives. At some point, we have all felt caught in the rat race where we wake up, go to work and repeat the cycle every week, every month, every year. It can be soul destroying when you're caught in the rat race and you feel you have nothing to look forward to. Even worse, when you can't afford to pay for the things you enjoy. Often, they can be very small, but because they mean so much they become significant and, therefore, non-negotiable.

For example, I love the movies; I am a massive fan of the Marvel Cinematic Universe, so the idea of not being able to watch the next *Avengers* movie or check out a new film every week is out of the question for me. It's how I escape and tune out of my busy schedule. My Odeon membership is an essential within my non-essentials.

In your life and finances, you are bound to have certain things that are essential in your non-essentials, and I encourage you to note them down in a hierarchy of importance. These can be hobbies or something you find fascinating. When you do this, think practically and realistically.

TASK 3

Make a list of all your non-essential expenses and mark any expenses that you feel could be considered an essential for you. Be honest in this, but don't overdo it. You only have two things. What will they be? Take five minutes to decide now.

If, for example, you love to keep fit and the thought of cancelling your gym subscription is a non-starter, allocate money intentionally to this each month. Doing so will ensure you're spending your money on the things that matter to you and will help with your sense of wellbeing.

This part of your budget is about your wants rather than your needs. As human beings, it is natural for us to think we need more than we do. We like to explore, experiment, experience new things. It's part of our evolution as individuals. The biggest challenge I faced before mastering my budget was settling how much money I was happy spending on my wants. Even then, I had to consider how much I could afford and how much is reasonable. I had to apply some financial restraint, otherwise the impulsive spender in me would do what he used to do and spend £1,000 on a pair of boots.

If there is wastage in your budget, I can guarantee you'll find most of it here in the non-essentials. If you don't have an eye on this, it's very easy to lose track of where you're spending money and what you're spending it on. In 2022, I appeared as one of the presenters on *Secret Spenders*, on Channel 4. In almost every household we visited, I discovered spending on non-essentials that shocked the couples we worked with. From spending hundreds of pounds a month on Coca-Cola to hundreds of pounds on Amazon, it's commonplace in our finances. The crazy thing is that sometimes we don't realise what we're doing and to what extent we're doing it.

When I worked in Canary Wharf in 2014, I got to the stage where I needed to figure out how to plug the hole in my finances and why I was broke at the end of every month. I was earning okay money at the time, but it was the first time I properly sat down with my bank statements to figure out where my money was going. It turned out I was eating out a lot. These were spontaneous Wednesday nights at Boisdale's or Thursday nights at the Duck and Waffle. I was spending £400 a month on having a good time and doing what a young single city boy does. As good a time as it was, it was crippling my finances and taking away from what I wanted to achieve. The solution was to rein it in. I didn't completely cut out time with my mates and enjoying myself, but I said 'no' more often and I set myself limits and boundaries. It made all the difference.

So, the question is, what do you want to allocate to this part of your budget? This is where you allow yourself to have fun. What are the things that will stop you feeling as though you're waking up and going to work with no actual sense of work–life balance? Write down what those things are, how much they cost and add them up. You'll be left with a number. This number is a percentage of your income: that is your non-essential budget.

Key Points to Remember and Action

1. The biggest challenge faced before mastering a budget is settling how much money you are happy spending on your wants.
2. Prioritising your non-essential spend is a great way to place a hierarchy on the parts of your non-essential spend you consider to be non-negotiable.
3. If you made your list in Task 3, please remember that this list will change as you do, so make sure you review it regularly.
4. Keep an eye on what you're spending here. It's easy to lose track of where your money goes.

CHAPTER 4

OTHER POT

Two defining moments from my time in Canary Wharf changed my outlook on how I interfaced with money. I use the word 'interfaced' because until then my interaction with money was robotic. So much so that I spent £1,000 on a pair of Giuseppe hi-tops without a second thought.

The first defining moment was in the middle of the summer on a Friday afternoon on the fiftieth floor of One Canada Square. You could see across London in all directions on a clear day from the office. My side of the office looked over East London, with uninterrupted views into the Olympic Village, and if you looked across the city, you could see the Wembley arches. The view never got old. Fridays were typically dress-down days, but I had clients in for meetings, so I was in my usual business attire.

After we concluded our meetings, I caught up with a colleague and, in small talk, asked what he was up to for the weekend. He said he was going to his home in Cornwall with his wife. I knew he had a property in London, but the second property in Cornwall surprised me. I knew he and I were earning about the same, but he had a different outlook on how he saw and used his money. I left that conversation embarrassed. I stood in a very expensive suit, designer shoes, with no appreciating assets to my name. A penny dropped.

The second moment was in the last few years of my time in Canary Wharf. My manager asked me a question in a one-to-one which put things into perspective. He asked what I was doing 'this' for. He asked what my life goals were. Not business or career goals; my life goals. It was the first time I had someone in a professional role ask me that question. I was taken aback, but it opened into a conversation about what my utopia looked like.

The job in Canary Wharf was everything you would expect it to be. It was exciting, fast-paced, growling, stressful, and rewarding in many ways. For me, buying my own home always seemed far-fetched. I was once homeless. How could I go from that to owning my own home? In that one-to-one, my manager not only helped me to identify my financial goal of saving for a deposit so I could own my home, but also showed me how I could achieve it within nine months. The job was hard enough, so why not use it to reach a personal milestone?

Looking back now, it was the moment that tipped my perspective 180 degrees. I became more focused. I worked my socks off and was much more savvy and structured about my spending. Knowing that my goal was achievable was the spark that lit the fuse in me. He, as my manager, got the best performances of my career as a by-product of that conversation and subsequent ones, I ended up on the property ladder.

Reliving those moments for this book has been cathartic. I learnt one of my most important and impactful life lessons from my manager while in my thirties. It wasn't a lesson I could have learnt earlier from my family, and in my younger years I had no mentors to guide and nudge me in the right direction. It's why I do what I do, it's why I'm writing this book. So many of us have never had a mentor, coach or teacher to guide us and share their experiences of one of the most important aspects of our lives. We prioritise what we want over what we need and attach so much emotional and external validation to the wants, rather than the needs and what matters. I spent a lot of my money on things I didn't need so that people, my peers, my friends, would perceive me in a certain way. It was about keeping up appearances. In doing so, I allowed myself to be influenced by external factors that lacked substance or meaning. I fell victim to consumerism and as a result further lined the pockets of millionaires and billionaires at my expense, and in exchange for what? A fleeting moment of self-gratification.

This pot is where you make your dreams a reality. It's where you can make what you thought impossible, possible. It's where all your hard work comes to fruition, where you gain a sense of fulfilment and purpose. The 'other' part of your budget is where you allocate some of your monthly income to your future goals. In order for this to work, you must be in a position where you have some disposable income at the end of each month. This will not work if your essential and non-essential spend accounts for all or the majority of your income.

In Doug's case, he was focused and tuned in to the things that mattered to him and his family. When you think about it, it makes sense. How many people wake up every morning, head to a job they hate, and do not know how to escape the situation they find themselves in? I've been there. The boss, the job and the colleagues I had made me miserable. I lived for the weekends, woke up on Monday morning dreading the week ahead, only to do it all over again. It's a horrible way to spend time you'll never get back. Doug allocated a whopping 35 per cent of his income to his 'other' pot – it was about building financial security for him and his family, using the money he was earning to buy back time that he could use more purposefully with them. What does the 'other' pot in your budget represent to you?

You wrote your goals in part 3 of Task 1. The only thing left to do now is write the financial cost of your goal. How much do you need to save for that house deposit? How much do you need for that summer holiday? If you want to pursue something you're passionate about, how much do you need to do it? How much will the school fees for your kids cost in the future?

Once you have that number, what remains is to decide how much of your income you can allocate to this pot to move you towards your goal. It doesn't matter what percentage you allocate as long as you allocate what you can afford and what feels comfortable for you.

Key Points to Remember and Action

One of the defining moments from my time in Canary Wharf that changed my outlook on how I interfaced with money was my manager asking me a question in a one-to-one. He asked what my life goals were.

1. Define your life goals and document what utopia would look like for you.
2. Write down the financial cost of your goal. Once you have that number, you need to make a conscious and concerted effort to assign some of your disposable income to this goal.
3. You need to have disposable income for this to work. If you don't currently have any disposable income, that's okay; now you know that you need some. Go back over your essential and non-essential spend to see if there's any excess spending you can cut back on.

CHAPTER 5

MAKING IT WORK FOR REAL

A budget is meant to be flexible. It has to be a fluid, moving, working tool you use to direct your money to where it needs to be. By categorising your money into the three pots we've discussed, you will become more intentional in how you spend it. You will lay the path towards the things that matter to you and the goals you want to achieve. There are a few things you must remember.

BALANCE IS KEY

Your budget is not supposed to restrict you or feel restrictive. Yes, it might be tight, but you have total control. Make adjustments where you feel it makes sense. Sometimes you may have to cut out certain expenses in pursuit of the goals you've put on your timeline. Often there are compromises to be made; don't be afraid to make them when you think it's necessary. Your budget will evolve as you and your goals evolve, and it should do. As things flex and change around you, so will your financial requirements. Your goals might alter completely, and along with them your financial commitments. Your budget is not a static framework, it should be a living, breathing tool. Some months, your spending may fluctuate across your three pots. That's okay, as long as you know what's happening and why.

Always review your budget

I review my budget once a year. That's what works for me. Some people prefer to review theirs monthly, others every six months. Find whatever interval works for you and set a reminder. Grab your bank statements, direct debits and subscription lists and go through them. If you do this regularly, you will spot services or subscriptions that you're not using or don't need. I do this every year and always find something I'm not using.

Don't obsess too much about the numbers; obsess about the habit you're developing

Most people won't be in Doug's position to allocate 35 per cent of their income to the 'other' pot. This is unrealistic on average wages, but what matters isn't the percentage. It's the habit. If you can cultivate the mindset to allocate 10 per cent, 5 per cent or even 3 per cent of your income into your 'other' pot, you're forming a habit with compounding benefits. Early on, it may appear that 5 per cent isn't much, but as you earn more, that 5 per cent becomes bigger and the benefits of the habit grow likewise.

Let's put some numbers on this. Five per cent of £1,000 is £50. Fifty pounds saved monthly is £600 a year. Let's assume you keep this 5 per cent habit and earn £2,000 monthly. Five per cent is now £100 saved monthly and £1,200 a year. Focus on the habit of saving a percentage and not the monetary amount. I had this realisation in my mid-thirties, and it's one thing I wish I had grasped in my mid-twenties. It's a small but immensely powerful catalyst to creating financial security and becoming your own financial hero.

Your mindset as you tackle this will determine the outcome

If you want to become your own financial hero, you must have the right mindset and motivation to develop and embed this habit. If you think it's a waste of time, then you are wasting your time. William H. McRaven, an admiral in the US Navy, once said: 'Want to change the world? Start by making your bed every day.' Budgeting is making your bed. If you're reading this and are willing to challenge yourself, it will transform your life, as it did mine.

Your 'other' pot is more important than you think

If you are driven, motivated and in tune with forward momentum, achieving goals and living with purpose, then the 'other' pot should be your top priority. If there is one thing you take from this part of the book, it's this.

When your budget is dialled in, you will find yourself in a completely different headspace. You will feel a better sense of control over your life holistically. This doesn't happen overnight, and I would never promise it will, but the payoff for your commitment is huge. Of course, this doesn't remove or do away with all of life's pressures, but it helps you feel more secure and prepared for the unexpected.

'Old habits die hard'

The biggest challenge you will face while embedding the practice of this new habit is the draw of old habits. Old habits die hard; this is precisely why we spoke about mindset and motivations earlier. In part 3 of Task 1 you were asked to document your goals and aspirations on a timeline. There are a handful of things you should look out for that could be signs that your budget isn't working and may need adjusting.

1. If you feel that your budget is restricting you, it's a sign that you need to get the balance right. A word of warning here, though: as humans, it's common for us to conjure up reasons not to do something. We convince ourselves it isn't working because it's uncomfortable, and it's not uncommon to feel like this, especially when changing our finances may involve certain sacrifices or a change in our habits. You must be honest with yourself. Is it your budget, or are the implications of change making you uncomfortable? Ask yourself the question and wait for an honest answer.

2. If you genuinely feel restricted by your budget, then you have to go back to the drawing board. Instinctively, you will know where you need to make changes. You may have to adjust your spending allocation to one of the three pots we've been discussing. For example, take back from the 'other' pot to give yourself more in the non-essentials to keep you motivated, or take from your non-essentials to add more into the 'other' pot so you can achieve your goals sooner. The decision is yours to make, and whatever decision you come to is the right one, as long as you're

being truthful and honest with yourself. The worst thing you could do here is cheat yourself of the goals you documented in part 3 of Task 1 of this book.

3. If you overspend in any of your pots, it's another sign that you probably need to get the balance right. We want to get to where the allocations you assign to each of your pots are sustainable and functional. We're looking to develop and embed a long-lasting habit that you can build upon. In the early stages, you may need to fine-tune this a handful of times, but the sooner you get to a practical allocation that works, the sooner you will be on your way to achieving your goals and becoming your own financial hero.

'Budgeting has only one rule:
Do not go over budget.'
Leslie Tayne

Equally, you should pay attention to your budget as a whole. If you find yourself overspending in one of your three pots it's an easy fix. However, if you're overspending across your entire budget and all three pots, you need to start again. The challenge here will be to bring your budget back into balance. This might mean making cuts. If you find yourself in this position, begin making cuts from your 'non-essentials' and 'other' pots first. If you still need to balance your budget, you will have to make cuts from your essentials. This can be painful, particularly if you have a family and some items on the chopping block are things for the kids or stuff that you consider important. These are often the toughest decisions to make, and some people can't make that decision. I have seen families go into debt as a result. Sometimes it's for a family holiday. Sometimes it's for the family pet. This can lead to a precarious mental struggle where the head-versus-the-heart equation leads to emotionally irrational decisions. Sometimes the heart will win, but it's a slippery slope when you continually allow your financial decisions to be led by your heart and not your head.

There are many reasons why budgets fail despite a well-intentioned beginning. It's normal to have a momentary inspiration that spurs you into action, but it's also normal for motivation to wane. That's precisely when you need something more to keep you going. New Year's resolutions are the perfect example. Every year we feel motivated, but statistics show that most people who set New Year's resolutions give up after six weeks. I want to put you on the path to success, so let's go through some of the reasons why budgets fail so you can identify them early.

WHY SOME BUDGETS FAIL

Unrealistic budgets

Most budgets are doomed to fail from the beginning because they are not realistic. We live in the real world, where things move quickly, and anything can change. Your budget has to be as flexible as the world around you. This means being honest with how you have allocated money to your pots. Wishful thinking or hoping for the best is the wrong approach. Your budget must fit your lifestyle and your unique set of circumstances. It shouldn't be shoehorned into place. It's like a glove.

Your budget should go hand in hand with your ambitions and lifestyle.

Speaking of ambitions ...

Not having a goal

This is a big one and one I've tried to address in taking you through this book to becoming your own financial hero. But the key to success in any endeavour in life is consistency. Your goals are the things that will keep you going. When you want to quit, think about the goals you set in part 3 of Task 1, go back over your notes and reflect on what your goals mean to you and how it would feel if you failed at them. You are more likely to be consistent with goals that motivate you intrinsically. These are goals that are linked to an internal driver instead of an external factor like looking good or impressing people. Getting on the property ladder or saving for your child's education are great intrinsic goals.

Not recognising small wins along the way

Sounds trivial, but I make a point of recognising the small things that validate any changes I've made and the small milestone I make when working towards my goals. I also practise gratitude, which I believe is one of the best habits you can develop. It helps me appreciate not only the big things but also the small ones. The small things don't get enough recognition. It's the accumulation of the small things that amount to the big things, and too often we forget to bask in the glory of the small things when they happen. For example, your goal may have been to save towards a house deposit. You should recognise and celebrate the first £100 or £500 you save as much as you would the final deposit figure. Celebrate it, pat yourself on the back and reward yourself for reaching a milestone. Not only will this give you confidence and a psychological boost, it will also validate and affirm the new habit you're developing and help you embed it for the long term.

Not having controls in place

This is also a biggie. It's become easier than ever to spend money without giving it a second thought. With contactless payment, it almost feels like you're not spending money. In the UK in August 2022, there were 2.1 billion debit card transactions, 6 per cent up on the previous year. Those 2.1 billion transactions amounted to £64.1 billion. That's a lot of coin. If your budget is to be successful, you must have controls in place to reduce unnecessary spending.

Call me old-fashioned, but I still use cash occasionally. I take out a certain amount of cash, and that has to last the week. If I run out mid-week, I can't use my card, and I can't take out any more cash. It helps me be more aware of my spending. It feels very different spending physical cash than tapping to make a payment. The psychology of spending money by using contactless payment is very different and it's one of the reasons why companies prefer you to tap to pay. You are more inclined to spend more. Consider opening separate accounts, one for bills, one for spending. Each month you pay in the appropriate amount and spend accordingly. If your spending account runs out within the month, tough. These types of controls will keep you accountable to yourself and your goals.

Lack of commitment

Many people underestimate how much of a conscious effort making and sustaining changes to their budget can be. Like most things in life, meaningful change requires commitment and discipline. There will be temptations to have that night out, or meal out, that shopping trip, or takeaway, those spontaneous couple of pints or glasses of wine, all of which you haven't accounted for in your budget. What seems an innocent slip or concession to temptation lays the groundwork for further concessions and, ultimately, a lack of commitment. Finding balance in your budget ensures you don't tip the scales into over-indulgence. It's about the middle, where the scales are in harmony, pushing you closer to your goal.

TASK 4

If you haven't figured this out already, it's time to put everything we've covered into practice. Take ten minutes to go back over your income and expenses and allocate money across each of the three pots we've discussed. What percentage of your income is allocated to your essentials? How much to your non-essentials? And how much have you managed to allocate to 'other'?

If you've been able to allocate some money to your 'other' pot, congratulations. If you've been unable to allocate money, that's okay. It's a work in progress, but you should now have a reference point to work from.

Key Points to Remember and Action

If you can, lay the path towards the things that matter to you and the goals you want to achieve. Balance is key. Your budget is not supposed to restrict you or feel restrictive.

1. Make adjustments where you feel it makes sense. Your budget will evolve as you and your goals evolve and it should do, so always review your budget to ensure it continues to work for you. If you can cultivate the mindset to allocate a percentage of your income into your 'other' pot you're forming a habit with compounding benefits. Your 'other' pot is more important than you think. It's the pot dedicated to your goals and should be your top priority if you are driven and have clear goals you are working towards.

2. Look out for signs that your budget isn't working and may need adjusting.

3. If you feel that your budget is restricting you, it's a sign that you haven't got the balance right.

4. If you genuinely feel restricted by your budget, then you have to go back to the drawing board. In the early stages, you may need to fine-tune this a handful of times, but the sooner you get to a practical allocation across your budget that works, the sooner you will be on your way to achieving your goals and becoming your own financial hero.

5. If you still need to balance your budget, you will need to make cuts from your non-essentials first and move to your essentials if necessary. These are often the toughest decisions to make but remember they are temporary changes for a bigger cause.

In a worst-case scenario, you may have to delay contributing to your 'other' pot until you have your essentials and non-essentials under control.

6. Most budgets are doomed to fail from the beginning because the budget itself is not realistic. Your goals are the things that will keep you going. When you want to quit, think about the goals you set earlier, go back over your notes and reflect on what your goals mean to you and how it would feel if you failed at them.

7. Recognising small wins along the way sounds trivial, but doing so is vital to the journey. It's the accumulation of the small things that amounts to the big things, so don't forget to bask in the glory of the small things when they happen.

8. If your budget is to be successful, you must have controls in place to reduce unnecessary spending. Many people underestimate how much of a conscious effort making and sustaining changes to their budget can be.

PART 2

A: AVOID DEBT

Debt is one of those things that we accept as a natural part of our existence. It's everywhere. Our economies are built on it. We run our finances using it, and the numbers are mind bending.

Here's a snapshot of the current state of debt in the UK.

The total average UK household debt was £65,346 in August 2022 (data from UK Debt Service).

Three hundred and thirteen people per day were declared bankrupt or insolvent in England and Wales from July to September 2022 (data from UK Debt Service).

Borrowers paid £135 million in interest per day in August 2022 (data from UK Debt Service).

The Citizens Advice Bureau dealt with 2,058 cases every day in the year to September 2022 (data from UK Debt Service).

Over 27 million adults in the UK are struggling with some form of debt (data from MoneyNerd).

As a nation, the UK's national debt currently stands at over £2.5 trillion. That's £2,500,000,000,000. We pay over £71 billion in interest annually, with interest accruing at over £2,200 a second. The level of debt we have as a nation is 118 per cent of our gross domestic product, or what the country brings in. We are in a debt crisis.

Many of us start our journey with debt at a young age. My first encounter with it was when I was nineteen – an overdraft facility that gave me a 'lifeline' if I needed it. That thing became a noose around my neck for fifteen years and a gateway to other forms of debt, like credit cards. If I could hop into the DeLorean and change anything, this would be one of the first things I would change.

When I started flirting with debt facilities such as my first overdraft, I wasn't mature enough to understand what I was getting into. I certainly didn't ask the right questions, and if I'm honest with myself I fell victim to fallacy thinking. Fallacies are mistakes of reasoning, as opposed to factual mistakes.

I was told that the overdraft could give me a lifeline, should I be in a position where I needed money in a pinch. In my head, this seemed like a good idea. I was still that kid who returned with £50 in his pocket. I knew the feeling of being broke and destitute. What harm could having a 'lifeline' do? I had no family I could turn to if I needed financial help, so this overdraft facility sounded logical. My thinking wasn't what it should have been. I didn't ask the right questions. What happens if I go over my overdraft limit? How much interest will this cost me? If I'm in my overdraft and go over my overdraft limit, are there additional charges I might have to pay? What are the overdraft charges, and how do they work? Twenty-four years later, those sound like reasonable and prudent questions to ask, but I didn't and here's why.

First, it was all new to me. I thought an overdraft was just something you have as an adult entering the world. I had no financial education or experience dealing with a bank, so when a bank offered me something, I took it. They had my best interests at heart. That's what I thought. I thought they were trying to look after me. I was as naïve as I'd been when I got on the plane with £50 in my pocket. I was wide-eyed, innocent, ill-prepared and foolishly wishing for the best.

Second, I didn't know how to manage money, which was the issue. I was still unfamiliar with the fact that bills were due at different times of the month, and that I therefore had to manage my money accordingly and plan ahead. I knew I had this 'lifeline', so when a bill was due that I hadn't planned for, the 'lifeline' bailed me out. And this is where I had the rude awakening. The overdraft facility bailed me out for a bill I hadn't planned for, but now, when I got paid, my pay was reduced by the amount I had used in the overdraft. Yes, I know you're probably reading this thinking, DUH!!! But it came as a complete surprise to me.

> **'Every time you borrow money,**
> **you're robbing your future self.'**
> Nathan Morris

The problem with debt is that if you don't have a plan, it becomes a compounding problem. I know that now, twenty-four years later, but at the time I wish I had someone to sit me down, slap me in the face and tell me to wake up and smell the coffee. I wish I'd had someone to talk me through everything we will cover in this chapter. If I could go back in that DeLorean, I would sit myself down and drill into lil' Pete's head that debt is a drain on your income, meaning the more debt you have, the less choice and freedom you have.

When you think of debt in that way, it takes on a completely different meaning. It doesn't seem as attractive or logical. If given the choice a rational person would presumably, in more cases than not, say no to debt rather than yes. It makes you stop and think. Is that car you're eyeing up worth robbing yourself of future income and opportunities for? Is that holiday you can barely afford really worth the chains of a nine-to-five you hate but have to stay at because you need the money to pay for the holiday later? Be honest, if debt was presented in this way, would it be worth it?

So why do people get into debt? There are many reasons, some of which you may recognise and relate to. Some have certainly been true for me. People fall into debt because they can't make ends meet. Usually, their income is less than their expenses, which leads to credit card and overdraft usage. People get into debt because they don't have a budget. People get into debt for social acceptance (wanting to be liked or wanting to fit in) and due to financial emergencies.

According to a study by financial comparison experts money.co.uk, in 2021 80 per cent of adults in the UK had debts. Disturbingly, the study found that 35 per cent of people's debt was largely due to 'normal' living expenses. Not emergencies or other unforeseen circumstances, but normal living expenses (essentials). This is a testament to the difficult times we live in but also a glaring indictment of the lack of financial education we have received. To compound this, perhaps debt has been too easy to access. Getting the first credit card might be difficult, but once you're in, you're in. I have witnessed so many stories where credit card limits are automatically increased, people receiving multiple offers for new credit cards and balance transfer offers through marketing campaigns by the credit card providers and the banks. In recent times, due to historically low interest rates, debt has been incredibly cheap to access, which has fuelled an increase in personal debt. In August 2022, consumer credit (individual debt through credit cards and personal loans) came in at £1.2 billion, according to the Bank of England. That's the figure for one month!!

This might seem innocent enough, but it feeds the narrative that the banks and the powers that be want us to be enslaved to debt. Just look at the numbers. According to the UK Debt Service, the Citizens Advice Bureau deals with 1,988 debt issues every day. That's 516,880 such issues over the 260 working days in 2022. This is a huge problem; and we haven't even spoken about what debt does to you personally.

WHAT DEBT DOES TO YOU

The impact of debt on us as individuals isn't spoken about openly enough in my opinion. It's only recently that we, as a nation, have started to acknowledge the debt issue and how it affects millions of us. We take a British 'stiff upper lip' approach to money in general, let alone something many associate with shame.

Throughout my twenties and thirties, I struggled with debt. I never spoke about it. I put it in this little black box and flung it into the deepest, darkest corner at the back of my mind. Like many people, I felt ashamed about my debt. In more recent years, I started wondering why we feel so ashamed. It's not like we're taught about this in school, so how are we supposed to know any better? We have this notion that we're supposed to make sensible financial decisions because we're adults. Again, I ask why?

Through my career in financial services, I noticed that most people access debt when there is a need for it. This presents a problem, because how can you make a lucid, rational decision when you have a pressing need for the facility you're applying for? To begin with, there's already a fear of rejection at play, so by the time you pluck up the courage to apply for the facility you need, the only thing you're hoping for is a yes. If you get that yes, you're so relieved that you immediately go into problem-solving mode and the fine print goes in the bin. A survey of one thousand credit card holders in the UK by price comparison expert Money Guru found that only 9 per cent of people understand their credit card agreement, and 64 per cent don't even read it. So, does this come down to a dereliction of duty by the banks and credit card providers or wilful ignorance by us, the consumer? There is an onus on both parties, but that's another debate entirely.

Debt's real impact on millions isn't just confined to our credit score. The real damage is what it does to our mental health. According to a study by the Royal College of Psychiatrists, half of all adults with a debt problem also live with a mental illness. Debt can make you anxious, leading to low mood, depression and stress. When I was struggling with debt, it was all-consuming. I suffered from incredible anxiety.

Whenever the phone rang, and it was a withheld or unrecognised number, I'd panic. When a letter came in the post, I'd panic. It was a horrible place to be, and for me it led to even more unhealthy behaviour that made the problem worse. In behavioural finance terms I fell victim to the 'ostrich effect', which is a cognitive bias that describes how people avoid negative information when facing a problem. Instead, we bury our head in the sand, which is exactly what I did. I couldn't face up to the problem because of the anxiety and shame I felt.

We need to speak about this ugly side of debt more openly. There are millions of people struggling with debt and mental health issues because of the situation they find themselves in. The problem is getting worse as multitudes across the country struggle to make ends meet. Prices keep going up, and wages are falling or stagnant. The situation is untenable.

CHAPTER 6

GOOD AND BAD DEBT

Not all debt is bad, and not all debt is good. There is an argument that all forms of debt are bad, but it depends on utility. We will need both types of debt at some stage of our lives, and understanding which type is which is crucial to making an informed decision.

Good debt is often debt taken out to purchase things, assets with the potential to increase your net worth or enhance your life. An example of good debt would be a mortgage. Most of us will find it impossible to buy a property outright with cash and so a mortgage is a great way to access the money needed, with the agreement that the money will be paid back over time. If you purchase a property using a mortgage, you would expect the property to increase in value and increase your personal net worth. Another example of a good debt is a business loan. If used properly, a business loan can help grow a business, which generates an income, which can enhance your life and lifestyle. Other examples of good debt are student loans. In specific fields where specialist qualifications are essential, a student loan to gain those qualifications would be considered good debt.

Bad debt is the opposite of good debt. Bad debt typically involves borrowing money to purchase things that depreciate or whose only purpose is for consumption.

I had a friend once who epitomises how not to use bad debt. He was very bad with money, even worse than me back in my late twenties. I remember this friend, let's call him X, taking out personal loans to satisfy his addiction to trainers. He would literally buy every variation of the Adidas Stan Smiths or Superstars he could find. He had a mountain of these things, unworn, unboxed, piled up in his bedroom. They were his pride and joy. He was a true sneaker head who ended up with hundreds of pairs of trainers mostly bought via debt. Needless to say, his use of bad debt didn't end there and, for years, he struggled with repayments. The last I heard, he ended up filing for bankruptcy.

Bad debt can extend to all sorts of things, but one of the most common forms found today is car finance. I have certainly fallen into this trap over the years. Who doesn't like a nice car, but, broadly speaking, most cars will depreciate in value the minute you drive off the car lot. In most cases, you pay a large deposit and commit to monthly payments over a term. In 2016, I remember putting a five-figure deposit down for a Tesla Model S. The car finance payments were more than my mortgage payment. At the time of writing this I still own the same car, but the truth is I could have allocated that five-figure deposit towards something that would have made me money instead of cost me money.

Determining what is good or bad debt isn't always as clearcut as you might think. It really depends on an individual's personal circumstances, what you can afford and why you're taking out debt. For example, you may be in a position where you need to pay off some existing debt and a consolidation loan may be appropriate. In this instance, it would enhance your life by reducing your monthly debt commitments, making consolidation a good debt. The question to ask yourself is, does this put me in a better position financially?

Most bad debt has a negative impact on our mental well-being. According to the Money and Mental Health Policy Institute, 46 per cent of people with debt problems also have mental health problems. This certainly resonates with me. I struggled with debt for fifteen years, and, as mentioned earlier, I remember feeling an overwhelming sense of anxiety whenever my phone rang from a withheld number or any time a letter arrived.

Studies by the Money and Mental Health Policy Institute found that 63 per cent of people with mental health problems found it harder to make financial decisions. This was true for me in my struggle with debt. I buried my head in the sand and avoided the issue because of how anxious it made me feel. It felt like I had Mount Everest in front of me and I wasn't equipped to tackle it. I consider myself lucky: twenty-four years later, I'm in a very different place. I have no debt aside from a small mortgage and I have escaped the anxiety. The reality is very different for others. Research shows that people with problem debts are three times more likely to have thought about suicide. Over 100,000 people attempt suicide while in problem debt each year. As problems go, this is a pretty big one and one we need to get ahead of.

TYPES OF DEBT

Broadly, there are two main types of debts: secured debt and unsecured debt. Within these there are also two sub-types that we'll touch on a bit later.

Secured debt is debt that you take out with some kind of collateral for the loan. An example of this is a mortgage. If you're unable to make the repayments for your mortgage, the house acts as collateral for the money you owe your lender. The lender repossesses your home as a way to recover the money they lent you because the debt is secured against the value of the property. Car finance is another example of secured debt. However, cars depreciate in value, meaning the lender may not always recover any outstanding debt fully if the person taking out the loan defaults. It's why you see better rates offered for a mortgage than for a car. So, from a lender's point of view, the risk of writing car loans is much higher than for a mortgage.

Unsecured debt isn't secured against the value of anything. Such debts are typically your personal loans, credit cards, overdrafts, payday loans and store cards. Because these types of debt are riskier for the lender, the interest rate and therefore the monthly payments are often more expensive.

I struggled with unsecured debt for years, and many people still do today. In fact, it's the most common type of debt. According to records, the total amount of unsecured debt in the UK in 2022 is over £300 billion. This averages out at around £11,000 per household, with unsecured debt growing at a rate of £80 million a day. Of that growth, 75 per cent is distributed across car finance, credit cards, overdraft and student debt, but here's the kicker. The age group using unsecured debt the most is twenty-five- to thirty-four-year-olds, who have five times more unsecured debt than older borrowers and are therefore far more likely to need to use credit to purchase essential items.

Now, I am writing this in the middle of a cost-of-living crisis in the UK, but these findings speak to a larger issue of how ill-prepared we are as a nation and how reliant we are on debt. It also lays bare the fact that generations of people have missed out on financial education. The chickens are finally coming home to roost.

There are two sub-types of debt I want to highlight before we move on. We will circle back to these when we talk about how to tackle debt should you be struggling right now.

The first sub-type is open-ended (revolving) debt. These will be things like your credit cards, store cards and overdrafts. These sort of credit facilities don't have an end date in sight. They are constantly available to you to use when you need them. On the one hand, this has the advantage of making funds available to you should you find yourself in a pinch, but there is another side to the coin. If you are unfortunate enough to be at the limit of your credit card like I used to be, paying off the card can be a struggle.

Here's what happened to me. Some of this might sound familiar.

I knew I'd maxed my credit card limit. I also knew that I couldn't afford to pay the full balance off in one go, so I resorted to the minimum payment. Now, on the surface, this is good. I'm not missing payments and I've set up a standing order to make the payment, so I'm never late. Great! But no, it's not great. In fact, it's the opposite of great. It's tragic. For two years, I made the minimum payment and then I suddenly realised that I hadn't paid off any of the balance I owed because the minimum payment only covered the interest. How could I not have known this? Well, I didn't think to ask at the time, because I was naïve. This is the danger with open-ended debt. Be responsible with its use and always have a repayment plan in place. The banks want you to make the minimum payments. It's great business for them because the interest goes straight to their bottom line. These types of debt will often have high rates of interest, meaning that it costs you more to keep and service them.

The second sub-type is closed-ended debt. This will be things like personal loans, car finance or anything that has a term to it. The benefit of closed-ended debt is that you have the comfort of knowing that the debt and its interest are fully paid off at the end of the term and you are free of that debt from that point onwards. With closed-ended debt, your monthly payments are usually fixed, which can be great when you're budgeting and structuring your finances.

Personally, I've always found this kind of debt easier to manage than open-ended debt. There's less to think about, and although the monthly payments are fixed and you don't have the luxury of paying a minimum payment, mentally I had a better sense of control and therefore, more peace of mind. Naturally, you may feel differently based on your preferences, habits, outlook and financial situation. What's important to note is how your preference leans to the options that are available to you and making an informed decision from there.

Key Points to Remember and Action

1. Good debt is often debt taken out to purchase things, assets with the potential to increase your net worth or enhance your life. Good debt can include:
   - business loans
   - student debt
   - mortgages.
2. Bad debt typically involves borrowing money to purchase things that depreciate in value or whose only purpose is for consumption. This will include:
   - overdrafts
   - credit cards
   - payday loans
   - store cards
   - personal loans.
3. According to the Money and Mental Health Policy Institute, 46 per cent of people with debt problems also have mental health problems. As such, it is crucial that we are aware of our situation and avoid burying our heads in the sand. This will only do more harm than good.
4. If you have open-ended debt like credit cards and overdrafts, you must have a thought-out plan to manage the debt effectively.

CHAPTER 7

INTEREST RATES AND DEBT

In my younger years, I was quite naïve about money and how the financial system worked when interacting with banks. As you can probably tell, asking the right questions wasn't my strong point, and that was because I didn't know the right questions to ask. It goes back to that saying I mentioned earlier: 'You don't know what you don't know till you know you don't know it.' I knew nothing back then, and I thought any question I might ask would be stupid. It's the age-old fear of being laughed at. Nobody wants that, so I didn't ask questions. I learnt the hard way that overdrafts and credit cards aren't free or cheap. When I finally realised they charge you interest, I still didn't understand how it all worked. If I had that DeLorean, I would certainly go back and ask about interest rates and how they work.

There is a charge for borrowing whenever you borrow money, be that as a mortgage, personal loan, overdraft, car finance, store card or payday loan. It's called interest. Interest is how the banks or the lender you've used make money.

Looking through history, it's common to have periods of low and high interest rates. Back in the 1970s, interest rates were high. You may have family members who recall paying 12 per cent interest on their mortgages. For the past thirty years, interest rates of that level have been unheard of, and in most recent history, we have enjoyed historically low interest rates. This is because central banks like the Bank of England have kept rates low since the last financial crash in 2007 and 2008.

Central banks control the interest rates we pay. In the UK this is via the Bank of England's base rate, which influences the rates commercial banks like Barclays, NatWest and Lloyds charge their customers for credit facilities such as personal loans, credit cards and mortgages. When the Bank of England base rate is low, our interest rates are low. When the Bank of England base rate rises, the interest rates we pay also rise. For the first time since 2007, the Bank of England has recently increased the bank rate several times. This means that the cost of using credit facilities has also gone up.

The interest rate you pay will depend on several factors: the type of debt you are applying for, the amount you are looking to borrow, the time you want to borrow over and your creditworthiness. We will speak about creditworthiness and credit scores later in this book.

An example is appropriate here. Say you want to take out a loan to purchase a new car for £15,000. A loan is a form of secured debt, meaning the car could be repossessed if you cannot keep up your payments, but as previously mentioned, cars depreciate in value. This means there's a greater risk to the lender, meaning the interest rate you will be charged will be higher than that of a mortgage where the house is collateral (houses typically appreciate in value).

A typical loan term is anywhere between one and seven years, so when you apply for this loan, the quote you get may look a little like this:

Amount borrowed: £15,000
Loan term: 5 years
Monthly repayments: £294.84
Interest rate: 6.9 per cent APR (representative)
Total amount repayable: £17,690.40

Many lenders will use different words to describe the cost of borrowing. The most important number to pay attention to is the APR. The APR for this personal loan is 6.9 per cent.

APR stands for annual percentage rate, which is the total cost of borrowing for a year, including any fees and the interest you'll pay. Occasionally, you may find that the interest rate and the APR differ. If they do, the interest rate will be shown separately and will not include any charges incurred for offering the loan.

Whenever you search for a loan, you'll notice that they are shown with a representative APR. Lenders have to use a representative APR because not everyone gets the same interest rate. A representative APR means that at least 51 per cent of customers receive a rate that is the same or lower than the representative APR shown. If you're looking for the best loan rate on the market, the representative APR is great for comparing the interest rates on offer.

When you apply for a loan and you've gone through the entire application process, you will receive a personal APR based on your circumstances. A big contributing factor to the personal APR you are offered is your creditworthiness: your personal track record of repaying your debts and keeping up with your financial commitments. If you aren't good with money or have a questionable track record of paying back your debt, such as having missed or late payments, the APR you will be charged will be higher. You'll get a lower APR if you have an excellent track record of repaying your debts and no missed or late payments. In short, the higher the interest rate you are offered, the more expensive are your monthly costs; conversely, the lower your APR, the cheaper they will be. You want low rates. The lower the rate you can get, the better. If you have a terrible credit history, the bank or lender may even decline you because they deem you too high risk. This can be extremely frustrating, particularly when you have a pressing need for the facility you're applying for. I've been there so many times, and with hindsight I realise that being declined for various applications I made helped me avoid sinking further into debt. I certainly didn't see it that way at the time, though.

In the example above, the cost of borrowing £15,000 to purchase a new car includes £2,690.40 in interest. It will cost £294.84 a month, which is a fixed amount for the duration of the repayment term of five years. This is a closed-ended debt facility, meaning that the loan and its interest will be paid in full at the end of your agreement.

Interest rates work the same regardless of whether you're taking out a car, mortgage, credit card or payday loan. It is worth noting that payday loans tend to have extraordinarily large APRs and therefore cost much more. They've had a lot of bad press in recent times due to this fact, and should be avoided at all costs.

A key lesson that's stayed with me over the years is how bad debt can affect you when you use it irresponsibly. It reminds me of Voltaire's quote, famously spoken by Uncle Ben in *Spiderman*: 'With great power comes great responsibility.' The decision to use credit should be one that is taken with careful consideration. It would help if you thought about how you will afford to service the payments beyond the immediacy of the next few months. Most people fall into problems with debt because unforeseen circumstances arise, and their circumstances change. You might lose your job, be made redundant, fall ill and find you cannot work. There might be a cost-of-living crisis that squeezes your income and hikes other bills you have to pay. If these circumstances came to pass, how would you cope?

Key Points to Remember and Action

In recent years, we have enjoyed historically low interest rates. This is because central banks such as the Bank of England have kept interest rates low since the last financial crash in 2007 and 2008.

1. The age of low interest rates is quickly coming to an end. This means that using debt or any form of credit facility is going to become more expensive. Consider how you will cope with repayments in a worst-case scenario.

2. The interest rate you pay will depend on several factors: the type of debt you are applying for, the amount you are looking to borrow, the time you want to borrow over and your creditworthiness.

3. If you're looking for the best loan rate on the market, the representative APR is great for comparing the interest rates on offer. You'll be offered lower interest rates if you have an excellent track record of repaying your debts and no missed or late payments. You will be offered higher interest rates if you have a poor track record.

CHAPTER 8

DON'T LET DEBT CONTROL YOU

In January 2022, 2.5 million households in the UK defaulted on their debt repayments. In February 2022, there was a 61 per cent annual increase in people taking out debt relief orders. These things are often last-resort measures people take because they cannot cope with the pressure of the debts they face.

Across the UK, we have seen an explosion in enquiries about individual voluntary arrangements. While these kinds of services are seen as a get-out for many people, the impact on their future prospects is not to be taken lightly. Bankruptcies can prevent you from being a director in your own business and stymie any other entrepreneurial aspirations you might have. These debt arrangements remain on your record for five to six years and will significantly affect your ability to get car finance, a mortgage or start a business in the future. That's not to say it's impossible to recover from using such mechanisms. You can. But it's likely to take over a decade to get back to neutral ground starting from zero again. We have a full chapter on credit scores and how these work later in this book, and you will be astonished at what information gets captured and how it can negatively affect your future prospects.

The consequences of using debt irresponsibly aren't solely financial. As previously noted, there is a mental health and time cost to pay as well. Dealing with debt is stressful. In my case, it kept me up at night, it was a cause of constant worry and, ironically, the longer I ignored it, the worse it got.

When you're under financial pressure, your ability to make sound financial decisions becomes impaired, especially if you become depressed about it. Instead of having a clear head to dispassionately assess the situation in front of you, the very thought of doing so can lead you to bury your head in the sand. This is precisely what happened to me. My overdraft was so big that it didn't matter that I got paid. I was constantly in the minus. Add my credit card debt to the mix and it was overwhelming. By burying my head in the sand I thought I was doing myself a favour, but I was causing more damage.

Even worse, I had no one to ask for help. I couldn't turn to my family in Nigeria, I couldn't ask my foster parents and I didn't have any family in the country to fall back on. I was on my own – a lone wolf. I had no previous experience of what I should do and no one to guide me, so I was making it up as I went along. In hindsight, all the mistakes I made put me on the path to writing this book and what I do for a living now.

HOW TO TACKLE DEBT

So, how did I tackle my debt? This may be the question at the forefront of your mind. If you are struggling with debt, it is vital to acknowledge that you need help at the earliest opportunity. As humans, though we may realise this, we often immediately dismiss it with a 'nah, it's okay' response. This happens in a split second and often subconsciously. Don't let it. Acknowledge and accept your need for urgent help. It's the early warning sign that the problem needs your attention.

There are a couple of things that stop people from tackling their debt head-on, or at least these were the two things that stopped me. The first was shame. I was embarrassed about where I was, the situation I found myself in, how I got there and how I allowed it to happen. I was an adult. Adults are supposed to make good, sensible decisions; by all accounts, bad decisions got me into this mess. I was scared about what these admissions would say about me, the choices I had made and how they made me look as a person. This sense of shame is common among many of us who have and are struggling with debt. Sure, we should know better ... or should we? Like you, I was never taught about money. I was never taught about debt, interest rates, the good, the bad and the consequences. So why should I have known better?

It's akin to this idea of playing chess for the first time against a grandmaster without a basic understanding of the rules of the game. You would be delusional to think you could win. The same applies to every aspect of money, especially debt. Most of us are not equipped with the skills and information needed to be in with a chance of winning. No wonder people sometimes feel as though the system is rigged against them. Why, then, do we feel ashamed about debt? Why is it so difficult to put up our hands and ask for help?

The second thing that kept me from tackling my debt early was knowing who to go to for help and how to approach it. I had this idea in my head that asking for help would be too complicated, and I didn't even know where to begin. Remember, in the early 2000s we didn't have smartphones, nor did we have social media talking about money and debt as openly as today. You had to make an appointment to see someone, which was scary. Today, help is a Google search away, and people like myself are online sharing their stories and experience and opening up the conversation. There were no non-profit organisations such as StepChange, founded in 2011, dedicated to helping people who are struggling. The resources we have at our disposal nowadays are vast and easily accessible. They make it easier to access help and, importantly, offer a more human approach. If you are struggling with debt, please contact StepChange or a similar organisation, but here are a couple of ways you can tackle debt that have worked for me in the past.

Debt prioritisation

You first need to understand what debts you have and how big or small the problem is. This needn't be complicated, but you must set aside time to do it. I estimate it will take you about ten minutes of your time to get an overview that will put you in a position to move forward. This is the first step when facing the problem head-on, and it will be challenging, but there is light on the other side. Doing this made me feel incredibly anxious, but by the end I felt relief and I better understood the challenge I was facing. Here's what you need to do.

TASK 5

Grab a piece of paper and write a list of all your debts: the outstanding amount owed and the interest rate. If you have credit cards, you need the name of the card (Barclays, for example), the outstanding balance, the interest rate associated with the credit card, and your monthly payments. You need the same information if you have a personal loan, car finance, store card, payday loan or overdraft. If you have a date when the facility will expire, like a personal loan, note that too.

Let's look at an example.

ADB store card – £125.96
Payment – £15.55
Interest rate – 9.7 per cent
End date – Not applicable (open-ended debt)

XX car loan – £12,852.64
Interest rate – 6.5 per cent
Payment – £325.85
End date – 25/07/2026

KCN credit card – £15,127.56
Interest rate – 32.5 per cent
Payment – £252.88
End date – Not applicable (open-ended debt)

XYZ credit card – £2,545.13
Interest rate – 8.99 per cent
Payment – £75.38
End date – Not applicable (opened-ended debt)

YXO personal loan – £3,412.68
Interest rate – 12.4 per cent
Payment – £183.41
End date – 12/03/2025

In this example, there are different debts. First, we have two closed-ended debts in XX car loan and YXO personal loan. They're closed-ended because they both have an end date – 25/07/2026 and 12/03/2025 respectively.

The second type of debt on this list is three open-ended (revolving) debts in KCN credit card, XYZ credit card and ADB store card. These are open-ended because they don't have an end date like the two loans listed.

The debts with the highest interest rates on this list are KCN credit card, YXO personal loan and ADB store card, in that order. When you prioritise your debts in this way, you can quickly see which debt is costing you the most in interest. Remember, interest is how the banks make money. It's a cost to you and the goal is to reduce that cost. There are several ways you can approach this, but this is how I would do so.

The highest monthly payment on this list is the car loan, which is £325.85 a month. This is a closed-ended debt with a clear end in sight. The same applies for the personal loan with the second highest interest rate and a monthly bill of £183.41. These two combined come to a monthly bill of £509.26. The open-ended debts (KCN credit card, XYZ credit card and ADB store card) don't have an end in sight. They are interest bearing and, combined, come to £343.81 a month in repayments. The approaches you can take to tackle these are many, but an important consideration to what's right for you will be your income, expenses, disposable income and, most importantly, how you feel about each of these debts.I prefer the structure and the knowledge that a loan will be paid off by X date. Knowing there isn't an end in sight with a credit card gives me anxiety. This is because of my experiences. That said, there is always a scientific or logical way to approach this type of problem, but you have to make sure that your decision feels right for you. You may decide to tackle the credit cards and store card, leaving the personal loan and car finance to run their course. You may decide to tackle them all at once. This is personal finance, so make sure you're making the best decision for you. Here are a couple of things you might consider.

Consolidation

Debt consolidation can be a powerful tool for an immediate reduction in the monthly costs of your debt. So how does it work? It does so by moving one or multiple debts into a single more affordable plan. Remember, credit facilities like overdrafts and credit cards are open-ended debt. They have no term, therefore, no end date. If you have multiple credit cards and an overdraft, it may be beneficial to consolidate the amount you owe into a personal loan.

You could bite the bullet and consolidate these debts into one personal loan and, therefore, one monthly payment. To consolidate all these debts, you could take out a new loan for £33,938.01. This does not include the outstanding balance on the ADB store card. It would make sense to pay this off as it's such a small amount; it wouldn't make good financial sense to add this to the new loan and pay interest on it.

The credit cards would be easy to deal with. Assuming you get accepted for a new loan, you would pay off each card when the loan amount hits your account. The car loan and personal loan would need careful consideration, as most lenders will apply penalties if you choose to pay off your loan early. You may leave both facilities to run their natural course. If you were of this opinion, you would need a consolidation loan of £17,672.69. This would move the credit cards from an open-ended debt structure to a closed-ended one. In doing this, you should end up with lower monthly payments, but that depends on the interest rate of the new loan and the term you choose to repay it over.

Back in 2017, I met a couple, Mary and Adam, battling with credit card debt. They had about £40,000 in credit card balances and couldn't see the light at the end of the tunnel. After years of only being able to afford the minimum payments, they finally explored debt consolidation options.

For Mary and Adam, we consolidated all their credit cards onto their mortgage. In their case, they had sufficient equity in their property to do this, and mortgage rates were lower than those of a personal loan; it meant we could save them £400 a month. If you consolidate onto a mortgage, it will probably cost you more in the long run. This is because mortgages have longer terms than personal loans, where the maximum term you can opt in for is usually seven years. Suppose you have fifteen years left on your mortgage when you consolidate. You're effectively adding the amount to your fifteen-year mortgage, and, despite the mortgage rate being lower than for a personal loan, the term means you pay more interest in the long run. Of course, this potential outcome would be different if you only had a short term left on your mortgage. The monthly payment will be higher but the interest in the long run will be less. In many cases, consolidating onto a mortgage can reduce the immediate monthly payments you make to your debts. For many people, this offers financial relief and an opportunity to bring their finances back under control.

You also have the added risk that if you don't keep up your payments, your home could be repossessed. This is an important point for anyone who is looking to consolidate onto their mortgage to ponder. Some people like this, others don't. It's ultimately down to preference and your circumstance. Seeking professional advice from a mortgage adviser will help weigh the pros and cons and determine the best decision for you.

Balance transfers

Balance transfers allow you to transfer the balance you owe on one card onto a new card on which you pay no interest for a prescribed period. That could be twelve months, eighteen months or twenty-four months. During the period in which you pay zero interest you can make strides in paying down your outstanding balance.

Keeping with our example above, you could consider a balance transfer to get as much of the money owed on the credit cards and store card onto a nought per cent interest rate. If successful, you could continue to pay off the card balance monthly but have all of your monthly payments go to the outstanding balance, not interest. The difficulty many people face when doing this is that they may not be able to transfer the entire amount they owe across multiple cards.

In our example, the card with the highest interest rate and the highest balance is the KCN card with a balance of £15,127.56. You may only get a balance transfer approved for £10,000, which doesn't cover the entire balance, nor does it account for the XYZ credit card with a balance of £2,545.13. It's not the perfect solution 100 per cent of the time, and it's why most people consider consolidating onto a loan, as there can be a better chance of acceptance. In this instance, I would still advocate paying off the ADB store card because it's such a small balance and an easy way to give yourself that psychological boost of paying one of the cards off.

If you can't transfer the full amount from the old KCN credit card to the new card because you're not accepted for the full amount, you may opt to transfer what you are offered. This would mean you will have to continue making payments to both cards. The good news is that £10,000 of the balance you owe will be interest free on the new card, but the remaining balance on the old KCN credit card will still attract the original 32.5 per cent rate you had previously. Your focus should be to pay off the balance on the KCN credit card as quickly as possible because it's interest bearing. While doing this, you should pay at least the minimum payment or as much as you can afford on the new card. Once the KCN credit card is paid off you can then focus all your attention on paying off the balance on the new card by the time your nought per cent period ends. It goes without saying that you will also have to maintain the payment on the XYZ credit card.

These kinds of balance transfers are a great tool if used correctly, but, as you can probably guess, I didn't use them correctly. Here's one mistake I made that ended up being quite costly.

Though I completed a balance transfer to a new nought per cent card, I didn't destroy the card I made the transfer from. Writing this now, I know it sounds stupid, and I was stupid, but this was my rationale: I'll keep it just in case I need it. Naturally, something happened where I didn't have any spare cash a few months later, and I resorted to using the card and compounding my debt problems further because I now had two credit cards to service. It's easy to convince yourself to keep your old card, but the best advice for anyone using balance transfers is to destroy the card you transfer the balance from. You don't want to leave yourself open to temptation, especially when you're an impulsive spender like I was.

MISTAKES TO AVOID

They say prevention is better than cure, so I think it's worth highlighting some of the bad habits/mistakes that got me into debt (apart from naïveté) so that you can learn from them.

Inability to manage money correctly

The catalyst for my debt problems was my early inability to manage my money correctly. It all started with an unaccounted-for bill paid for using my overdraft, and that was it. An innocent mistake that spiralled into a much bigger problem spanning fifteen years. Just so there is no confusion, the lesson here is to ensure you have reasonable control over your finances with a budget. If you completed Task 4, you should now have a clear picture of how your budget is working. You've started to lay the foundations.

Using debt to get out of debt

This is technically possible, but you must have a plan to make it work. I thought it would be a great idea to take out a credit card to bring down my overdraft. BIG mistake. In my naïveté, I paid the overdraft using my credit card but didn't get the overdraft taken off my account. I don't need to tell you what happened next. Take a guess. I had another bill I hadn't accounted for, and there I was, back in my overdraft, only now I also had a credit card to pay off. Please don't make this mistake.

Not automating payments to my debts

We all get busy with day-to-day life, and it's natural to miss things, but missing your repayments is not worth it. If I could have my time again, I would automate my payments. Setting up standing orders to pay your credit card is simple and easy to do. It ensures you don't have to remember the due date or to make payment. It's a no-brainer.

Using credit cards and overdraft facilities as an emergency fund

I used my credit card and overdraft facility as an emergency fund. While it might seem like a good idea, you will almost certainly end up in the same place as I did. Additional unforeseen costs can send you into a downward spiral in a flash. It is always best to build an emergency fund over time. By doing so, you will cultivate healthy financial habits you'll be thankful for.

Burying your head in the sand

When things got terrible, I struggled. I didn't face the problem head-on. Instead, I ignored all communication from the lenders and, worst of all, I lied to myself. It's easy to do. I told myself it would go away, and despite how severe a negative impact it had on my mental health, I doubled down. In the end, facing up to the problem wasn't as bad as I had built it up to be, and it was a relief when I finally did so.

Key Points to Remember and Action

1. If you're struggling with debt, it is paramount that you seek help as soon as possible. Organisations like StepChange are a great place to start.
2. Debt consolidation can be a powerful tool in bringing your debt under control. It's worth remembering that there are lots of options you could explore, but you should speak with a professional to help you arrive at the best solution for you.
3. A balance transfer is a great tool to help you manage your credit card debt and pay off your debt. The best practice with a balance transfer is to pay down as much of your balance as possible by the time your nought per cent period ends. If you can pay it off in full, even better, but please remember to always destroy the credit card you transferred your balance from.

PART 3
S: SAVE EARLY

For the longest time, I had a real issue with saving. I had poor spending habits, which led me to spend indiscriminately. I would see something shiny and instantly tell myself how good it would make me look and buy it. The absence of proper reflection meant I never developed a rational thought process. It was all emotion, and my emotions drove the habit that got me into debt. When you cultivate a spending habit for so long it becomes hard to break. It's a vicious cycle of doing the same thing repeatedly.

> **'People who want to kick their habit for reasons that are aligned with their values will change their behaviour faster than people who are doing it for external reasons such as pressure from others.'**
> Elliot Berkman, neuroscientist

Saving was never something that occurred to me. I couldn't escape the scarcity mindset that I grew up with, and no matter how many difficulties I had that told me I needed to change, I couldn't quite bring myself to do what I knew was necessary.

Neuroscientist Elliot Berkman said that people who want to kick their habit for reasons aligned with their personal values would change their behaviour faster than those who are doing it for external reasons such as pressure from others. This speaks to intrinsic and extrinsic motivations, and at the time, I had no intrinsic motivation to change despite the pain the habit was causing. I reckon the same is true for you and that's why Task 1 of this book is so important to help you drive change and break habits.

'More than one in four people have less than £100 in savings, one in six people have no savings.'
Money and Pensions Service

As a society, we have a problem saving. According to the Money and Pensions Service, over one in four people in the UK have less than £100 in savings, and one in six have no savings at all. Admittedly, numerous factors feed into this kind of data, but you must ask how this is possible and what we have to do to fix the problem.

In this social media age, never in history have you been able to connect with people so freely. It has always been challenging to connect with prominent celebrities or people you admire and aspire to. You now have a backdoor into the life they want you to see, the luxury cars, houses and holidays. Not only do we then use what we see as a barometer for what our existence should look like, but it drives the one thing that lubricates world economies and deepens the pockets of industry fat cats. Commerce is the exchange of goods and services. Social media is the new advertising space for brands and industry. When was the last time you used your social media account and didn't come across an ad selling you a product or service? Social media has succeeded in helping your favourite celebrity or influencer to achieve something brands have failed to do for centuries: making you care and feel connected. That's why brands spend millions on influencer marketing. They recognise the power of connection. It makes us even more susceptible to marketing efforts and makes us more of a slave to consumerism.

HOW MANY MILLIONAIRES ARE YOU WEARING?

When I worked in Canary Wharf, I had a conversation with someone who changed my perception and the way I think about things. They asked me how many millionaires I was wearing. I didn't quite understand what he meant when he asked this question, but he repeated it. How many millionaires are you wearing? It stopped me in my tracks because I had never been asked this before, and I didn't know if it was a trick question, so I asked, 'What do you mean?' He explained that every piece of clothing I had on, every accessory I was adorned with, was created by someone who built a business, to sell a product that made them a millionaire or billionaire. As what he said sunk in and I took a step back to think about it, I realised he was 100 per cent right. The pair of jeans I was wearing was from a company founded by someone who is now a billionaire or millionaire. The trainers I was wearing, the watch, the socks, and even my underwear were created by a business whose owners are millionaires or billionaires.

I remember the first time I spent a lot of money on a pair of trainers: my infamous Giuseppe hi-tops, a beautiful pair of trainers, but they cost me £1,000. I didn't think about spending that much; I thought about how buying them made me feel in the moment. I felt like I owned the world, and that's how these brands want you to feel. They want you to feel like you've conquered the world, as though you deserve this purchase. But what do you trade for that fleeting moment of invincibility? A thousand pounds of my hard-earned cash, which went to line the pockets of a millionaire who created that brand.

I'm sure you will be able to relate to this. You've probably bought something that's made you feel great for the moment, but you're overwhelmed by buyer's remorse shortly afterwards. After I had spent £1,000 to acquire those beautiful Giuseppe hi-tops, and after that initial rush of euphoria from my retail therapy dopamine hit, a feeling of regret and shame quickly followed. I could not bear the thought of returning to the shop to ask for a refund of my thousand pounds. As a result, I've worn those suede Giuseppe hi-tops in public about seven times, and they're still in their box today.

> **'I robbed myself of the ability to make my money work harder for me.'**

How many millionaires are you wearing? How many millionaires have you enriched by parting with your hard-earned cash for a fleeting moment of euphoria and satisfaction that ultimately is short-lived? Once the brand-new feeling has worn off, what are you left with? The same sense of emptiness that further spurs the spending habit in search of that dopamine hit. Reaching that point changed my perspective because I realised that this vicious cycle was robbing me of future prospects. It was robbing me of the ability to make my money work harder and, ultimately, my ability to become my own financial hero.

WHAT KIND OF SPENDER ARE YOU?

We can't talk about saving without talking about the other side of the coin. For every saver, there is a spender. Over the years, I've tried to understand the psychology around my old spending habits, and this is what I've found. It's quite fascinating.

In a 2007 study, neuroscientists found that spending has a perceptible effect on the brain. When we anticipate a new purchase, the brain receives dopamine spikes and the nucleus accumbens (the brain's pleasure centre) becomes more active. The researchers discovered that the dopamine surge the brain receives is even more intense when a bonus is involved; for example, a sale or buy-one-get-one-free offer. They also found that the prefrontal cortex and insula lit up when products were accompanied by their prices. These are the parts of the brain responsible for decision making and processing pain, respectively. From this, the neuroscientists surmised that when the brain's pleasure centres are more active than the pain centre, a person is more likely to make a purchase.

The researchers found that people enjoy shopping precisely because of the sensation of pleasure and reward associated with the activity. An issue arises when the satisfaction gained from spending isn't balanced by the pain of overspending; this can lead to a full-blown shopping addiction known as oniomania or compulsive buying disorder (CBD).

Oniomania is different to being a 'shopaholic', where you go on a shopping spree occasionally but have control over what you buy and how much you spend. Shopaholics can recognise and balance the pain of overspending and decide appropriately. Oniomania is driven by the urge to shop in search of that dopamine hit with a disregard for the pain of overspending. It can be a coping mechanism to fill a void or to distract from other issues elsewhere.

I'm not sure how I would diagnose myself, I'm not a professional, and, up till now, I never thought there could be an actual condition for the habit with which I was struggling. I now recognise that I had abandonment issues from my past, I desperately wanted to fit in at a place I felt I didn't belong professionally and I had all these unhealthy preconceived notions of what success looked like, not to mention a scarcity mindset. It was a recipe for disaster.

Spontaneous spender

I was then, and still am, a spontaneous spender. I see something, I like it, I buy it. I'm driven by the urge, a spontaneous impulse, sometimes at the expense of rationality. Knowing what kind of spender I am has helped me to understand myself better and to put in place mechanisms that help prevent me from spending in the way I used to.

I learnt that I would spend on a whim if I went to certain places, spent time with certain people or felt in need of a pick-me-up. In recognising these triggers, I was able to pre-empt any spontaneous spend. For instance, I would ensure that I didn't go to Selfridges when I'd just been paid or around bonus times when I was flush with cash. I would make sure that on a Thursday, if the boys wanted to go out, I would leave work early, or I would say no because I knew that on a Thursday night if we ended up in the Duck and Waffle, that was maybe a hundred pounds on drinks and food.

If I felt low, I would make sure that I didn't end up going to certain places or spending time with the people that would encourage my spontaneous spending.

If I did go to Selfridges, I would make sure that I didn't carry my cards with me. I would carry a small amount of cash. It's small interventions like these that made a massive difference to me.

Reward spender

You have spenders who like to reward themselves or reward people for good work. So, on reaching a milestone, you may celebrate and splash out. Such spending could be very unhealthy, but it can also be healthy if you're working towards a business goal and using it to spur you on. If you're working towards career goals, patting yourself on the back and rewarding yourself with dinner or an item you've always wanted is perfectly okay.

If you're a parent, you may reward your children for good exam results, good behaviour or when they do chores. This can have an immediate positive impact, but it can also be problematic because a reward is an extrinsic motivator and rarely leads to positive outcomes in the longer term.

Hurried spender

I am also one of these, where I will spend money if I'm under pressure and need something to be done quickly. A hurried spender is the type that makes purchases on impulse without much thought. The trouble with being this type of spender is that if you're in a rush, you often end up buying more expensive items or paying over the odds for a service because of time pressure. If you are a hurried spender, you're likely to be purchasing something on impulse; you leave yourself with no thinking time.

Payday spender

We all know someone who's a payday spender. When payday comes around this person will make a beeline for the shops to get that dopamine hit as soon as possible. This can be particularly tempting if you are in a stressful job or hate the one you're in. If you're a payday spender, you probably smash through your budget pretty quickly after payday and subsequently find yourself strapped for cash.

Bargain spender

Bargain spenders love a good deal. They go to town on the Black Friday sales, on buy-one-get-one-free offers, on 75-per-cent-off deals; such offers send them into a frenzy. This type of spender is more likely to spend because of the attraction of the offer and its impact on the pleasure centre of the brain.

There are more spending personalities than those I've just listed, but it is invaluable to know what kind of spender you are. All of these personality types are laden with positives and negatives. If you want to become your own financial hero, you need to identify which of these types applies to you, and logically and pragmatically put into place mechanisms that can inhibit the spending habit from negatively affecting you.

As mentioned earlier, one of the biggest mistakes I made when I started working in Canary Wharf was lifestyle creep – spending more as I earned more and not appreciating that, by doing so, I was digging a deeper hole for myself. At the time, I thought that because I was now earning more money, I could afford to go to better places and buy nicer things, but those things became more expensive to service. A prime example of this is upgrading to a better car. All of a sudden, car breakdowns cost more to service, tyres are more expensive, fuel is more expensive, and so it goes on.

> *'It wasn't until much, much later that*
> *I appreciated it's okay to lifestyle creep*
> *but important to be mindful of how*
> *much your lifestyle creeps by.'*

It wasn't until much, much later that I appreciated it's okay to lifestyle creep but important to be mindful of how much your lifestyle creeps by. I am in no way a frugal spending enthusiast. I think it's natural for us as human beings to want to do nice things, go to nicer places, wear nicer clothes, drive nicer cars and live in more exquisite homes. It gives us a sense of fulfilment, progression and achievement for all the hard work we've put in, but it is also essential to ensure that we are doing it within the confines of our budget.

There is no point in buying a £1 million house on an income that stretches you to the limit because you're in love with the idea of a £1 million home. That's how many of your favourite celebrities have ended up bankrupt. We must cut our cloth according to our means, and not succumb to social pressure or what we assume to be the expectations of the people or society around us. So, before buying that next car, ask yourself if you can afford it. Ask yourself if it's the best use of your money. Is it going to prevent you from saving? Is it going to stop you from doing other things financially? Could that money be better used to secure your future through becoming your own financial hero?

'Wealth is quiet, rich is loud, poor is flashy.'
Tim Denning

I don't want you to be in a position where you've bought a car, but you're still broke, struggling to make ends meet and now in debt because of the finance agreement you just signed. That isn't what you're here for. The goal isn't to be seen in the nicest car you can just about afford. It is to be financially secure. It is not about the flashy things, but about having peace of mind and security around your finances.

ALLOCATING CASH

As I've previously mentioned, your 'other' pot is where you can start to allocate money towards your goals. If you can't find some form of meaningful motivation to allocate money to your 'other' pot, then I have bad news for you. You will never be able to begin moving towards your goals. I've learnt this through many years of guiding people as a financial adviser, working with financial advisers and being around wealthy people. What I've learnt from them is the importance of formulating a specific plan for allocating cash. This is something your average person tends to miss and why the other pot in budgeting is so crucial.

The fact is that we can all save. Speaking from personal experience, though, I came up with plenty of excuses as to why I couldn't start doing so.

The first excuse I told myself was that I couldn't afford it. Things may have been tight, but in reality I could have sacrificed a night out with the boys, skipped buying an outfit for the weekend, and taken some homemade lunch to work instead of spending money on food at work. There were a host of things I could have done to reduce my outgoings and start to save, but I didn't have the willpower or the mindset to make it happen.

The second excuse I used was, 'I'll start saving next month.' Because money was tight, I couldn't face the idea of sacrificing something for the greater good. Procrastination kicked the can down the road, and one month inevitably turned into two months, two into three and three into six. Ironically, every time I procrastinated and delayed action, something else that I hadn't planned for would happen and worsen my financial situation. I would find myself going deeper into the overdraft, using more of the credit card balance, or seeking a new credit card because I'd maxed out on the one I already had. Procrastination compounds the negative impact of poor habits.

'Time will creep up on you like wrinkles.'

Another excuse I came up with was: 'I'm too young. I'll get around to it next year.' Again, another form of procrastination, but this is a common one among young people, and it still gets me. The biggest and most precious asset we have is time. Time waits for no one. If you stand still, it's moving on without you. By the same token, time will creep up on you like wrinkles. One moment you haven't got them. The next, they're there, and you wonder how and when it all happened. The younger you are, the more important it is to implement the habits that my B.A.S.I.C. formula teaches. As much as procrastination compounds the negative effects of poor habits, it can also compound the positive effects of good ones. When we come, later in this book, to consider the subject of investing, you will see how everything comes together to help you become your own financial hero.

The last excuse I gave myself was that I couldn't save because I was in debt. If I'm honest, this was probably the truest excuse. I was already in a pretty bad place because I had buried my head in the sand and couldn't see a way to make it work. At that juncture in my life, I would have benefited from a mentor to help me see the wood not the trees, but sadly that wasn't the reality.

CHAPTER 9

THE IMPORTANCE OF SAVING

Over these past couple of years of my being on social media – YouTube and Instagram specifically – I've noticed a narrative circulating that, for me, is counterintuitive. It started with the millionaire/billionaire influencers and, for some reason, is repeated and lauded as though it's gospel. It's a perfect case study of the power of social media, and how ideas and opinions can take on a life of their own and grow tentacles that extend and mutate.

Under any other circumstances and coming from anyone else, these ideas and opinions would be challenged and debated. Because their source is the super-wealthy, though, both practical and critical thinking go out of the window.

I understand the allure of these personalities online, and I also appreciate the desire to learn from someone who is where you want to be. However, there is something called 'financial planning', and most of these personalities have no financial planning experience.

As controversial as this may sound, the millionaires and billionaires in the financial space online are in a completely different arena to 99 per cent of the people on the planet. They are the 1 per cent who have access to a host of investment opportunities, have a completely different set of tax management issues and tools. These personalities have vastly different levels of cash, disposable income and, in most cases, multiple streams of income. Their financial standing means that they have access to the best advice and financial tools, to which the average person will never be in a position to gain access. In almost every instance, I would argue that their 'advice' on saving and money management is completely irrelevant to ordinary people. I did say it was controversial.

The narrative I hear that seems to be obsessively repeated is that cash is trash. They all say this for the effect and shock value, but is it really that shocking? The statement requires context because it is multifaceted and nuanced.

'Cash is not trash for people who are building the foundations needed to take the next step into wealth creation.'

Cash is not trash for people building the foundations needed to take the next step into wealth creation or to stabilise their current finances. Everybody wants to create wealth, and everybody wants to put their money to work, but you can't walk before you crawl, and you most definitely shouldn't jump out of a plane without a parachute.

We need to address the purpose of savings and the role they have to play in helping you become your own financial hero. These online millionaires and billionaires will have you believe that cash is trash and that you should not hold money in cash. They claim that you should ensure that every penny is working for you, and there is some truth to this, but not if you don't have an emergency fund in place, not if you're struggling with debt and not if you can barely make ends meet. This is the role your savings can fill, and it's an essential component of the foundations we have spoken so much about. The bottom line is, if you can't budget or have the discipline to maintain a budget and you can't make responsible decisions with cash, you will never be able to create financial security. You will never become your own financial hero.

The obvious rebuttal to what I've just outlined is that your money is wasted in cash because ten pounds today isn't going to be ten pounds one year from now, due to the increase in the cost of goods and services around us (inflation). The other argument against cash is that interest rates do nothing to help you keep up with inflation, so you're resigning your cash to lose value. If you follow logic, you need to have your money in a place that gives it the biggest chance to match the cost of things increasing in price around us. This is correct.

Inflation in 2022 is at levels we haven't seen since the 1970s, and interest rates are comparatively low. This gives very little incentive and return for people looking to hold their money in cash. In a perfect world, your savings rate would match the prevailing rate of inflation, which would be sufficient to maintain the value of your savings and round the equation.

As I write this, we're in the middle of interest rate rises, so savings accounts are starting to become more attractive, but they are still some way away from levelling the playing field for savers. This means that there remains a disparity between inflation and rewards for saving, which bolsters the argument of the super-wealthy against holding any cash. The argument, however, skips over the fundamental reasons why we save in the first place.

WHY YOU NEED TO START SAVING

We've already observed that one in four people in the UK have less than £100 in savings and one in six have no savings at all. We have noted that if you have money worries, you are 4.1 times more likely to suffer from anxiety and 4.6 times more likely to experience depression. With those numbers in mind, you cannot underestimate the psychological comfort you'll get from having a healthy amount in cash as a safety blanket. For most people under financial pressure, the psychological relief of having a safety net far outweighs the disadvantages of infla-tion. Even if you are not under financial pressure, having a healthy amount in savings is crucial for your sense of financial security. It is equivalent to the parachute on your back in a skydive. You would rather have it and not need it, than need it and not have it.

Savings are essential for everyone, and here are a few reasons why you need to start saving ASAP.

1. It helps you avoid debt
Debt is a drain on your income both now and in the future, and it's an expensive way to fund purchases because of the interest rates associated with the different types of debt facilities. Bad debt, in particular, can set you back years if you don't start out with all the facts and the money management skills required to manage your finances after you've taken out the debt. Saving

can help you plan ahead for purchases that you may or may not know are coming down the track, and it can help absorb the impact of any sudden financial shocks that often lead people into debt.

2. It gives you peace of mind

I'm conscious that I've repeated this so many times already, but that's because of how powerful it is when you're trying to navigate life daily. Most of us have business pressures, career pressures, family pressures and personal pressures. The one thing we could do without are unnecessary financial pressures, especially when we can do something about them. Saving will help you sleep better, feel better and make you feel more confident in your endeavours. When you start to build your savings, you will free up vital mental space, which can lead to less stress and anxiety. You can start to move forward into a better personal and professional space.

3. Saving can help you escape the rat race

I am an example of how putting savings in an emergency fund can unchain you from the restraints of a nine-to-five job. Most people who have managed to break away from a nine-to-five say it's one of the best things they ever did, and I agree. Having an emergency fund has been the catalyst for a more fulfilling and rewarding life. It has enabled me to do things I could only have dreamt of just three years ago. Having sufficient savings to cover your essential bills could be the difference between continuing in a job you hate and transitioning to something more rewarding.

4. It is a springboard to help you reach your financial goals more quickly

Most people will have to find a way to finance their goals and aspirations from their income, and saving is the first step in making that happen. For example, if your goal is to buy a property, you first need to save for your deposit. The same applies to most goals that people set; saving is how you assign your money to your goals.

BREAKING OLD HABITS FOR NEW ONES

It's really important we go back to something previously touched upon about identifying and understanding what kind of spender you are. I shared with you earlier that I am and will forever be a spontaneous spender. Over the years, I have put in mechanisms that have helped break this habit. That isn't to say that I'm frugal or I don't indulge and enjoy the things that bring me joy, but what I've been able to do is find a balance.

If you identify as one or a combination of the types of spenders outlined, you must find a way to break or at least manage the triggers that set off the habit. To break a habit, it's important to identify the causes that lead to it before replacing them with a new desired behaviour. I was able to identify my triggers through journaling and being aware of the fact that I might have an issue. Once I identified my triggers, a pattern started to emerge, and I could put in place mechanisms that helped me. If you know what kind of spender you are or if a number of the spending profiles resonate with you, here are some suggestions that might work for you.

You may be a hurried spender, where spending is a way to fix something quickly because you are under pressure, or where it is based on impulse. A solution to this may be to pre-plan what you must do and prepare yourself beforehand. If it is a case of quick purchases, give yourself a time rule before you buy something. It could be a five-minute pause and check-in, giving yourself the time you need to collect your thoughts.

If you are a spontaneous spender like I am, identify the triggers that get you to spend. Is it a particular place you go to? Is it particular people or friends? Is it a specific time of the month or year? Is it a certain mood or emotion that gets you spending? It could be something as simple as wanting to cheer yourself up or to feel better about yourself. Identifying these things will help you avoid them. If you're a bargain spender, then things like Black Friday, Black Monday, Christmas sales or any form of sales will likely trigger you. In that case, you may decide not to have access to Amazon on Black Friday. Restrict your social interactions, so you don't receive the stimulus that could trigger you. Alternatively, you might decide to be pragmatic and give yourself a set budget to spend.

Whatever approach you choose to tackle your spending habit, it's important that it's practical and you have some way of holding yourself accountable. You need to cultivate a new set of habits that will serve you better than the old ones.

This is the real reason why saving is so important. You must muster the discipline required to structure your finances in a way that is conducive to saving towards your goals if you are to become your own financial hero. Otherwise, you will never be able to free yourself from debt, and you will never be able to escape the rat race of the nine-to-five.

Saving is like the ground floor above the foundations of the Shard. It's the reception area you walk into before ascending to the other floors. It's your reception area from which you can start building different aspects of your life.

I am a prime example of what is possible when you save and create a financial blanket around you. It has been the stepping stone that has put me on the road to everything that has happened to me subsequently and everything I do now on TV; to you reading this book, and everything I've done online with my podcast and my YouTube channel. You can do this too, as we will discuss next.

Key Points to Remember and Action

Take what you hear online from social media personalities with a pinch of salt, especially when they are unqualified. There is a lot of good information online; however, it's important that you retain your ability to think critically. The millionaires and billionaires in the financial space are the exceptional 1 per cent. As such, their financial landscape is nothing like yours.

1. Cash is not trash for those building the foundations needed to take the next step into wealth creation or stabilising their current finances. Holding reserves of it is a crucial habit to cultivate.
2. Savings are essential for everyone.
3. Saving can help you plan ahead for purchases you may or may not know are coming down the track, and it can help absorb the impact of any sudden financial shocks that often lead into debt.
4. Saving is the best way to finance your goals. It's the first vital step you have to take.

CHAPTER 10

EMERGENCY FUND

Let's get real. One of the core functions of having savings is to give you a financial blanket, that sense of security over the unexpected should anything come down the path in the future. Your ability to deal with financial shocks is one of the key pillars in your financial wellbeing and, as an extension, your mental health. Saving towards an emergency fund ensures you're not using the debt facilities we covered in the previous chapter that could cost you a lot of money and stop you from having peace of mind in the long run.

'When it comes to an emergency fund, everyone should have one.'

Many people ask me how I've created an online business that has led me to do national television and write this book. The truth is, I would never have been able to give this my undivided attention had I not had a healthy emergency fund to cover essentials and provide a buffer. My emergency fund was the segue I needed to transition from my day job to my career and business, and this is what I want you to realise. An emergency fund isn't just a boring pot of cash. It's the doorway to what we aspire to in life, especially if you're looking for balance, choice, security and freedom.

I started my business at the beginning of 2020. I didn't know that the pandemic would hit in March 2020. But when I got made redundant from my position with a wealth management company, I decided that this was the time to give it everything. I had wanted to do this since 2017, but I didn't dare. I was shackled with golden handcuffs, so when the pandemic came around in March 2020, it was the perfect opportunity to give the business my complete and undivided attention. I had nothing to lose and everything to gain.

I was fortunate to have around £28,000 in savings, which I had set aside over previous years, to give myself an emergency fund for something like this. For a considerable time, I wasn't using the funds and felt like they were wasting away because of low interest rates. I felt I could make them work that little bit harder for me, but didn't want to lock them up because it's rare that you foresee an emergency coming before it happens. That's why it's an emergency. For me, peace of mind in the knowledge that I can access funds immediately outweighs any interest returns I might have earned in a bank account, especially in a low-interest-rate environment at the time. How you view this may be different, and some arguments will advocate for a different decision, but in my fifteen years working in financial services I've found one thing to be constant. The decisions we make about our finances and money are not always logical. I have had many instances where clients have ignored the logical thing to do and gone with an emotional decision because it felt like the right thing for them and their goals. It's the classic head versus heart dichotomy.

'It makes no sense that you would go to a job you hate, receive your pay cheque and fritter the money away without giving yourself an exit.'

Recent research from Gallup, a company that helps leaders, organisations and businesses solve problems, found that 85 per cent of people hate their jobs. Eighty-five per cent! To put this into context, according to the National Statistics Office, there are 67.6 million people in the UK. If we assume that 40 per cent of those are working adults, that would mean that 34 million people in the UK are currently unhappy with what they wake up to do every day – trapped in the vicious cycle of the nine-to-five. Many people in this position want to leave and bid farewell to their boss, but they don't have the financial means to do so. It makes no sense that you would go to a job you hate, receive your pay cheque and fritter the money away without giving yourself an exit.

When it comes to an emergency fund, everyone should have one. It's a signal of intent, a sign that you are being proactive, thinking about the future, and preparing contingencies so that you can pivot, protect yourself and put your best foot forward when an opportunity arises or when you decide it's time to make a change. It gives you choice and freedom. If I hadn't had my emergency fund when I needed it in 2020, I wouldn't be on national television, I wouldn't be writing this book and I certainly wouldn't be living my dream. I would be back in the corporate world, earning well but hating every minute.

Unfortunately, for many people, an emergency fund is seen as this unnecessary pot of money sitting there that may never get used. For a long time, I questioned what I was doing with mine. I hadn't needed to dip into it for a while and started wondering if I needed it. I started plotting what other use I could put it to; for example, what holiday I might take next, what investment I could put it into. These are all legitimate thoughts and questions, but this is where, psychologically, we fall victim to the gambler's fallacy. The gambler's fallacy is the incorrect belief that if a particular event occurs more frequently than expected in the past, it is less likely to happen in the future, or vice versa. So, in my case, if I hadn't needed to dip into my emergency fund for a while, it seemed unlikely I would need to in the future. You can see how that way of thinking is flawed. For many of us, the gambler's fallacy prevents us from taking action and lures us into a false sense of security.

An emergency fund doesn't have to be a quit-my-job fund. It could be a pot of money set aside to cover you when you need to replace the boiler, fix the car or anything that comes out of the blue as a financial expense. An emergency fund is not for retail therapy, nights outs, lunches, dinners or holidays. You must be disciplined in understanding the difference between emergencies and non-emergencies, because that will carry forward into how you deal with your emergency fund in the real world. If you're not clear on this, you'll cheat yourself and use excuses to let your discipline go. This will set you back and halt any progress towards your goals.

HOW MUCH DO YOU NEED IN AN EMERGENCY FUND?

This is the million-dollar question; as you can imagine, there are different answers to it. There is a mathematical answer, and then there is a more down-to-earth, real-world answer. I will take you through the mathematical answer first.

We discussed budgeting and your essential spending, allocating a certain amount to the latter. Your emergency fund could be a mathematical calculation of your total monthly essential spending times the number of months you want to cover. So, for example, if your essential spending (your rent, mortgage, gas, electric utilities, council tax etc.) comes to £1,000 a month, and you multiply this by the number of months you want your emergency fund to cover you for, let's say six months' coverage, you would need £6,000 in your emergency fund.

During my time as a financial adviser and now as a money coach, I've found that the number that people arrive at varies widely depending on their circumstances, the size of their household and a number of other factors. I've had clients who've wanted to have twelve months' worth of an emergency fund and others that only wanted three months'.

If you use this approach, you must think realistically and in a worst-case scenario. Such an approach means that you will get the most bang for your buck – i.e. the greatest amount of peace of mind – because you are using real numbers from your budget to create a safety net. Unless something changes significantly, you know you're covered for most eventualities.

The second way to approach the question is to ask yourself how much you want to have in an emergency fund to make you feel secure based on your circumstances. This number may differ from the mathematical number we came to earlier, but it is a starting point. Such an approach works well if you don't have a lot of disposable income. I coach many people and have found that starting with a smaller amount, such as £100 or £200, can be a real psychological boost. A hundred pounds can turn into £300; suddenly, you're en route to having one month's worth of essential expenses covered.

> *'It will be a process that will test your metal, challenge you, and make you question yourself and your habits.'*

Regardless of how you answer the question, staying grounded is important because your emergency fund number is likely to be pretty large. You'll probably look at it and think, wow, and that's okay. Knowing what you need is the first step, but action needs to follow. Remember, Rome wasn't built in a day, so you must appreciate that this will be a work in progress from the get-go. This will be something you work towards. Do not expect that you can create it overnight. It will be a labour of love. It will be a process that will test your metal, challenge you, and make you question yourself and your habits. It will be tough, but it's worth it once you get to the other side. What you will learn from breaking those habits and changing your behaviours is repeatable for other areas outside your finances.

WHERE'S YOUR EMERGENCY FUND COMING FROM?

Your emergency fund isn't going to magic itself out of thin air. It has to come from your income, and your disposable income specifically. In the budgeting part of the formula, your 'other' pot is funded from your disposable income. In turn, your emergency fund has to be funded from your 'other' pot. If you don't have sufficient income to allocate towards this, you will need to revisit your non-essential spending and see what could be reduced or cut to make this happen.

By now, you should have prioritised your non-essential expenses into a list of hierarchical importance (Task 3). If you've done this, you will have a list of non-essentials vital to this part of your budget. I gave the example that my Odeon membership is essential in my non-essential spending. This puts other things in my non-essentials on the chopping block before I consider cutting my Odeon membership.

If you've done the same, it will make your decision-making process less emotive and more logical. I'm not going to lie. If you find yourself in this position, cancelling things can be painful. It will shock your system, and you may start to question why you should continue with this. That's why we went through part 3 of Task 1, establishing your why and putting a flag in the sand to signify how soon you want to achieve your why.

There is no shortcut here, but if you try to bypass this, you'll only cheat yourself of progression and growth in the long run. If you have to make sacrifices, please remember that it's only temporary, and in the long run, you'll probably realise you never needed the things you cancelled and will value the sense of achievement and satisfaction you get as you progress towards your goal.

SAVINGS ACCOUNTS

One of the most common questions about saving is where should I put my emergency fund? This is a great question that often leads to debate. People start to weigh the options and the merits of their choices. I often point people back to a couple of key points that are important if they want to make the best decision.

An emergency fund is for emergencies, so this has to be at the forefront of your selection criteria.

Some people may hold different views, but the interest rate on your account should be the cherry on top of the cake, not the cake. In other words, focus on something other than the rate if it means you've got to lock up your money. That defeats the purpose of an emergency fund.

You will come across different account types when looking for a place to keep your emergency fund or any other savings you've managed. Let me give you an overview of the main account types you are most likely to come across (in the UK; similar accounts will exist in other parts of the Commonwealth).

Individual savings account (ISA)

ISAs were introduced in the UK in 1999 to encourage people to save more. They came with a promise that all money deposited within a set limit (called the ISA limit) would be tax-free for as long as the account was open and regardless of how much the account value ended up being. Since 1999, we've seen the ISA limit grow to £20,000 as of the time of writing this book.

An ISA is the first account you should consider for your emergency fund or any savings you hold. You can save up to £20,000 into the ISA every single tax year (between 6 April and 5 April the year following). Every penny you save is completely free from tax in the UK. This means no tax on the interest you receive.

Cash ISA

This is the go-to account for savers as it's low risk and instantly accessible. Suppose you're a saver looking for a place to allocate your emergency fund. This is the perfect account. You can open one of these with your local bank or building society. The interest rates on offer may not be great, but the real attraction of this account is its tax-free status.

Please note that there are specific rules on how to contribute to your ISA during a tax year. You want to ensure you stay within the contribution rules.

Easy-access accounts

This account does what it says on the tin. It offers instant access to the funds in the account at all times, allowing you to deposit and withdraw money with no restrictions or penalties.

The interest rates offered on easy-access accounts are typically the lowest on the high street.

Unlike an ISA, where the maximum amount you can pay in is £20,000 during the tax year, there is no maximum amount you can pay into an easy-access account.

NS&I Premium Bonds

NS&I (National Savings and Investments) is a UK-owned savings bank, offering Premium Bonds and a range of other savings accounts. NS&I Premium Bonds are one of the options available, and they are extremely popular.

NS&I Premium Bonds are tax-free, like an ISA, meaning you pay no tax on the interest you earn. The minimum you can pay in is £25 and the maximum is £50,000. Premium Bonds offer an interest rate, but this doesn't work like other savings accounts. The interest rate goes to fund a monthly prize draw. Prizes range from £25 to £1 million and all are tax-free.

At the time of writing this book, NS&I has awarded 4.9 million in tax-free prizes.

Premium Bonds do not offer the guaranteed return most saving accounts offer. However, the prizes you could win in the monthly draw are, as indicated, tax-free and a lot of people like the idea of being in with a chance to win £1 million.

Regular savers

A regular savings account is great if you want to build up your emergency fund or savings over time. It will typically require a certain number of regular deposits over a set period. This is twelve months for most accounts on the high street. A regular saver often has a maximum amount you can pay in each month; you can't simply pay in a lump sum when the mood takes you.

Regular savings accounts have been known to offer higher rates than an easy-access account, but it is worth noting that the interest you receive each month reduces with every contribution you make. Let's look at an example using a 2.5 per cent interest rate. If you save £250 a month into a regular saver, you will earn interest on the cash held each month. This means that the first £250 contribution will be in the account for the full twelve months, attracting £6.25 in interest. In turn, the second £250 saved will be in the account for eleven months, earning eleven-twelfths of 2.5 per cent (£5.73 in interest). This repeats every month for the duration of the regular savings account.

Missing payments to a regular savings account can lead to penalties such as a reduction of the interest rate being offered. Early withdrawals can be subject to similar penalties.

A regular savings account may not be a good fit if you're building your emergency fund or already have such a fund in place. The restriction on withdrawals and the limited monthly deposits could work against you. These accounts could work for people who want to start saving and are keen to get into the habit. A regular savings account is great for developing the habit because of the enforced regime of monthly deposits.

Notice accounts

These accounts require some advance notice to gain access to your money. In exchange for your giving notice, the account provider will typically offer a higher rate of return than for an instant-access account. Notice accounts will typically have different notice periods. This could range from a thirty-day notice to sixty or even ninety days. The number of days typically dictates the notice period required. For example, thirty-day notices need thirty days' advance notice to make a withdrawal. Longer notice periods often command higher interest rates, so a ninety-day notice will have a more attractive rate than a thirty-day notice.

Some notice accounts will allow you to access your money without notice, but you will have to pay a penalty. Typical penalties on a notice account are a loss of interest for the equivalent number of days' notice, such as loss of thirty days' interest on a thirty-day notice account.

There are advantages and disadvantages with all the accounts I've just listed, so be sure to be curious and ask questions to ensure you have enough information to make an informed decision. Please remember that one size doesn't fit all, and you may want to use a combination of these accounts. The most important thing is to take the approach that suits you and your circumstances. If you are confused, visit my website or find me on social media for further guidance.

Key Points to Remember and Action

Saving towards an emergency fund ensures you're not using debt unnecessarily to fund your livelihood. As we've already discussed, debt can be costly and stop you from having peace of mind in the long run.

1. When it comes to an emergency fund, everyone should have one. It's a security blanket to cover you for emergencies and a vehicle to help you move towards your goals.
2. Your emergency fund could be a mathematical calculation of your monthly essential spend and the number of months you would like your essentials to be covered for. This could be three months, six months or nine months. Alternatively, you could start with a much smaller sum. Ask yourself how much would give you a sense of security and work towards it.
3. Your emergency fund should be easily accessible. Do not lock it in an account that restricts your access. We covered earlier some account types that could be an option for you.
4. Building your emergency fund can seem like a daunting prospect, but it's a great stepping stone to much bigger aspirations and goals.
5. Your emergency fund should be funded from your 'other' pot. If you worked on your budget in Task 3, you should have a better bird's-eye view of your finances, which should help you to begin to move forward.

CHAPTER 11

SAVING ALONE ISN'T ENOUGH

Through my personal journey, I've found myself transitioning between different phases of wellbeing, financial pressure, stress and security. The thing that sticks out for me the most is the difference between the early days and now. Throughout my life there has always been some element of scarcity, be it from the mindset that was ingrained in me when I was with my foster parents, to the scarcity of electricity and running water in Nigeria, to the scarcity of shelter when I was homeless, to the scarcity of courage and capability I felt while battling with debt, to a scarcity of security, which made me feel as though my world could be swept from beneath me at any moment. It's a strange thing to try to describe, but I never felt immovable. I always felt like I was one pay cheque or one performance review away from my world crashing around my ears. I was in a constant state of fear and anxiety over the future. I don't know if most people feel this way, but it's exhausting. It constantly drains you of energy and peace.

I've come to realise that most of this fear and insecurity is down to my experiences, and my relationship with money. Thankfully, my time in financial services has done more than just pay my bills. It's given me knowledge, a shifted mindset, and it has transformed how I feel about and see the world. I no longer feel scarcity, I no longer feel movable, I feel secure, and saving has a lot to do with that. It has allowed me to put in place mechanisms that have helped to vanquish any lingering fears I once had about being homeless again. Saving is a fundamental part of the structure you need to have in place in order to become your own financial hero, but saving alone isn't enough.

'The role of saving is to keep you from being poor.'
Jane Bryant

The role of saving is to keep you from being poor. It never has been and never will be the vehicle that builds wealth in the long term. If you've come from a background similar to mine, not being poor might be a good enough outcome. It might even be your goal. In fact, I would argue that not being poor and having the financial stability to live life comfortably without the financial pressure of how you're going to cover your bills is a fantastic outcome. Being in the position where you can afford a couple of holidays a year, you have a decent amount in an emergency fund, you've got zero to little debt, you've got all your basics covered, should be the standard for all of us. This would make for a comfortable life that for many of us from poor backgrounds is a universe away from what we grew up experiencing.

Saving will help solidify your foundations, but it will not ensure you can retire early, it will not help you acquire a comfortable retirement, it will not create wealth that will give you the full range of choice and freedom you may be aspiring to. If you truly want to become your own financial hero and create the life of your dreams, you have to look beyond saving. Here are some reasons why:

YOUR MONEY NEEDS TO BE COMPOUNDING

Compound interest is another concept most of us didn't get taught in school that should be taught as standard. It refers to interest earning interest on itself. In order for your money to work efficiently and as hard as possible, it has to be compounding. Most savings accounts today will grow with compound interest, but the rates are too low to have a significant impact in snowballing your money for growth in the future.

Once you have your foundations in place – a robust budget, good control over your debt and a healthy emergency fund – this needs to become your next priority. If you have aspirations of a comfortable or early retirement, your money needs to be compounding. If you want to generate a passive income from your money, your money needs to be compounding. If you want to create generational wealth, again your money needs to be compounding. More on this in the next chapter.

INFLATION, INFLATION, INFLATION

Your money has to keep up with the cost of things going up around you, at the very least. It's acceptable to overlook this as you get your ducks in a row and create your emergency fund, but after that you have to start thinking more practically. Once your emergency fund is in place, the surplus cash you used to grow the emergency fund needs to be allocated to something that gives you the best chance to outpace inflation and grow your money for future use. This is how you start to create wealth and where you begin to have a serious conversation about where to put your money and how best to make it work for you. More on this, likewise, in the next chapter.

YOUR EARNINGS ARE SHRINKING

If you are in an employed role, it's likely you've seen very little wage growth in recent years. With the cost of most items increasing around you, the unfortunate side effect is that your earnings are shrinking as well. For example, if your rent or mortgage increased by 3 per cent this year and your earnings haven't risen at all, you've effectively seen a 3 per cent cut in earnings. In this instance, we've only looked at one crucial aspect of your expenses. In reality, the true extent of your salary shrinking could be much more pronounced if you consider other areas where costs are increasing. This is another way to look at inflation but with a focus on your income. The solution here is to earn more money and allocate what you can into something that has a real chance of outpacing inflation.

Key Points to Remember and Action

1. You need savings to create the foundation you need for a comfortable lifestyle; however, this is only the first step in a long journey.
2. Savings will help you solidify your foundations, but:
    *   they will not help you retire early;
    *   they will not help you retire comfortably;
    *   they will not create wealth sufficient to give you the full range of choice and freedom you may aspire to.
3. Most savings accounts today will grow with compound interest, but the rates are too low to have a significant impact in snowballing your money for growth in the future.
4. Savings alone will not be enough to accomplish the primary goal of keeping up with inflation so that your money maintains its value.
5. Once your emergency fund is in place, the surplus cash you used to grow the emergency fund needs to be allocated to something that gives you the best chance to outpace inflation and grow your money for future use.
6. Remember, savings will only keep you from being poor.

PART 4

I: INVEST EARLY

The last eight years of my career in wealth management were the most eye-opening. Wealth management is where I learnt completely alien concepts and the mysterious things you can do with money. It was the first time I had ever encountered the methods and principles of investing. During those eight years, I worked with financial advisers on numerous cases as a consultant, as well as for an investment house that built pension and bond products. Financial advisers would recommend these innovative solutions to their clients. We ushered in a range of investment products that guaranteed investment returns for future use. I qualified as a financial adviser in 2015 because I wanted to help clients plan and reach their financial goals in a tangible way.

This part of the B.A.S.I.C. formula is where I get to share and discuss what excites me and what I'm most passionate about after fifteen years in financial services. I started my business in 2020 with the mission to share everything I've learnt throughout my career in corporate and retail banking, especially wealth management, in an open, easily digestible manner. I learnt a lot about the ins and outs of how investments work.

I also learnt the impact they can have on consumers and how the things I was learning were inaccessible to ordinary people. I also learnt how the markets operate and how important investing is to our future aspirations of creating wealth and becoming our own financial heroes. It is the part of the financial services industry that excited me the most, and I want to share the key things I've learnt in this part of the formula.

INVESTING IS HOW YOU MAKE THE BIG THINGS HAPPEN

Investing is all about taking that next step to create wealth. This step truly matters if you are serious about becoming your own financial hero. Everything we have covered in earlier parts of the formula represents the foundations you need to have in place to make this part of the formula work. You cannot invest if you don't have an effective budget. You should not be investing if you are struggling with debt; you should not be investing if you don't have an emergency fund. Investing is how you make the big things happen. It's where you leverage the power of compound interest. Where you create and execute a plan to retire early, create financial freedom and build a life you can live on your terms.

It's time to look at what investing is. Let's talk about investing myths, why we invest, risk, risk management, investor psychology, how investments work, and how to start investing safely. It's also crucial to avoid certain mistakes when you begin investing to ensure you have the best investing journey possible. Investing is what I've been looking forward to discussing the most in this book, because it represents what I'm most passionate about and what has been most influential in my career thus far.

Over the years, there's been a lot of misinformation about investing. The banks, financial advisers and the investment industry have perpetuated a lot of this. It has been made to look more complex than it needs to be. Investing is fundamentally quite simple. Even a ten-year-old could understand the basics. If you can grasp the fundamental principles, the steps to start investing are straightforward, particularly nowadays when we have the benefit of technology that has revolutionised our ability to access markets.

Years back, when I was in my twenties, if I wanted to invest in the stock market, I would have required £5,000 to begin with, and I'd have needed to see a financial adviser to get started. Financial advisers were expensive and had a terrible reputation, some for justifiable reasons, others for reasons that weren't justified. I say this, being fully aware that I am a qualified financial adviser myself. The truth is that financial advisers have a role to play in financial planning and helping you structure your investments once you reach a certain level of wealth where their skill set and the tools they have at their disposal are warranted. For some people, that's £100,000. For others, it can be more or less. I will walk you through everything you need to know as a beginner to start your investment journey, beginning with the most crucial question.

WHAT IS INVESTING?

The Amsterdam Stock Exchange, created in 1602, was the world's first formal stock exchange, and it was set up so that people could buy shares in a company called the Dutch East India Company. It was the first time you could buy company shares, receive dividends and, in return, partake in a company's growth and profits. Unfortunately, that stock exchange has long since disappeared, but numerous other exchanges have taken its place, such as the New York Stock Exchange, the London Stock Exchange and the NASDAQ.

To understand what investing is, we must understand what a stock market is. The stock market is a market where you can buy publicly traded companies on an exchange such as those mentioned above.

WHAT ARE STOCKS?

Stocks are companies. Look around your home at your television, laptop, washing machine and microwave. Who manufactured them? Look at your phone. If you own an iPhone, the company that makes the iPhone is Apple. Apple is a company and, therefore, a stock, which you can invest in by buying a share in the business. By buying shares in a company like Apple you become a part owner (shareholder) in Apple, and therefore become eligible to partake in and benefit from the profits that Apple makes.

This is fundamentally what investing is all about. It's about buying shares and taking an ownership stake in a company or a group of companies that you believe produce great products and render excellent services that will lead them to be profitable in the future. Apple is the world's most valuable company. It has a net worth of two trillion dollars; that's two followed by twelve zeros. Apple has more money than some countries, and as an investment it has delivered phenomenal returns for investors since it first started trading on the New York Stock Exchange in 1980. An investment of £100 in Apple at the beginning of 2002 would have grown by more than 130 times its original value by mid-October 2019. In other words, if you had invested £100 in Apple at the beginning of 2002, by mid-October 2019 your £100 would have been worth £13,000. Wealth is created by investing in companies that make products and render services integral to our lives.

This is how wealthy people have created wealth throughout the generations, and the truth is that Apple is not the only game in town. There is a whole plethora of companies that you can invest in that are similar to Apple. They all make products and render services that are integral to our lives, and as you go about your day-to-day business, I encourage you to start looking at the items you pick up, the services you use and the things you buy. Look at the companies behind them; you will probably be able to invest in all of them.

According to the Coca-Cola website, over 1.9 billion Coke servings are sold daily. Coca-Cola's revenue (money made) in the twelve months to 30 September 2022 was $43.4 billion. Coca-Cola is an excellent example of a business you can invest in, and the list goes on and on across several industries. Think about telecommunications: Vodafone, AT&T and Verizon Communications. Or energy: Exxon Mobil, BP, Chevron. Investing is about being more than a consumer of products and services. It's about being a shareholder in the companies you are a consumer of. McDonald's, BP, British Gas, Sainsbury's, Ocado, Tesco, Rolls-Royce and Barclays are all companies you can invest in, building your wealth for the future.

WHAT INVESTING IS NOT

Over the past few years on social media, investing has been confused with something that it isn't, so we need to discuss what investing is not. Investing is not trading. I have witnessed these terms being used interchangeably by influencers who are pretenders. They have no qualifications and no real-life experience. They see the financial space online as an opportunity to make money and feed their ego. Investing and trading are fundamentally different. When you invest, you buy shares in a company like Apple with the view that it will be worth more than it is today over the next ten to fifteen years. As a function of its growth, your investment in the company will also grow, giving you a healthy return. This is a long-term position with a long-term view. Trading is quite the opposite.

Trading is the activity of speculating on market outcomes at any given time. A trade using Apple as an example looks like this. Is the Apple share price going to rise or fall today or next week? You place a trade betting on what you think will happen. If you are correct, you make money on the trade. If you're wrong, you lose money. It therefore becomes a rapid transactional activity. You're not taking ownership of any stock. You are not becoming a shareholder in the business. You are simply betting on the outcome of your assumption about a stock's share price. Trading comes in many different forms. You can trade stocks as described, but you could also trade cryptocurrencies, forex (foreign exchange) and even commodities like gold, silver or platinum. Trading is a high-risk game that requires a lot of experience, technical know-how and dedication. Across social media there are legions of accounts that profess to have simplified trading for beginners. They provide services that they claim make trading easy. The promise is that you can trade for twenty minutes a day and make life-changing money. Many will sell signal services that indicate what trades you should place and their possible outcome (they must have a crystal ball or a DeLorean to see into the future). Most of these services have been proven to be scams or money grabs for those who create them. The truth is, 95 per cent of retail traders lose money when trading, and no service you can subscribe to will lower those odds. It takes years of experience to be a profitable trader, and requires hard work and dedication. So, remember: if it sounds too good to be true, it probably is.

MYTHS ABOUT INVESTING

There have been many myths about investing. We need to understand these myths and debunk them. We also need to move beyond them so you can start investing with confidence. Here are the most common ones I've come across.

Myth one: you have to be rich

This may have been the case twenty to thirty years ago but that isn't so nowadays. In recent years there has been an explosion of new companies, allowing everyone to start investing with as little as £1. These companies are on the way to successfully democratising investing for ordinary people, which is a joy to see. They are easy to open your account with, easy to use and have an easy-to-follow process that guides you on making the right investment. Apps are available to download in all the app stores, meaning you can be up and investing in no time.

Myth two: investing is a quick way to make money

This is another lie that has been perpetuated on social media. Investing is now this sexy thing that results in Lamborghinis, flashy homes and luxury watches. It feeds into people's aspirations for a better life, into people's greed and into our innate desire to do as little as possible to make money. Who wouldn't want money to grow on trees, but, unfortunately, we know that such narratives are false.

Investing is not a quick way to make money; if anything it's slow, boring and steady. It's the art of creating wealth gradually by dedicating sufficient time to invest diligently and wisely. Investing is not and will never be a get-rich-quick scheme or a way to make easy money; in fact investing carries a risk to your capital. It is almost a certainty that you will lose money at some stage during your investing journey; as such, your mindset going into investing has to be right and you have to understand how you are going to manage and cope with investment risk.

Myth three: your money has to be locked away for the term of your investment

This is not true when you invest in the stock market. While you must take a long-term view (investing for at least five years), your investments have no lock-up clause. You can access your money at any given time, but there will be some considerations to determine if withdrawing your investment is the right thing to do.

Markets go up and down constantly, meaning that the value of your investment will fluctuate regularly. Many people who invest tend not to withdraw money when the markets are down. Instead, they may take money out when the markets are up, since it's likely that the value of their investment is also up. This keeps the original amount they invested intact and allows them to take profits over and above their initial investment.

Myth four: past performance guarantees your future returns

When you are investing, this could not be further from the truth. The markets have peaks and troughs. They have ups and downs, and past performance in the market is no indication of future performance.

When discussing risk management later in this chapter, you will understand how important it is to manage your expectations based on several factors. When you begin investing, it's important to note that your returns are not guaranteed. That's even more reason why it's crucial to make the right decisions at the right time and to begin investing in the right way.

Past performance gives us data that we can look back on to help us surmise what might happen next. This can inform the decisions we make but is not a guaranteed way of predicting what will happen in the future.

Myth five: investing is complicated

Investing is as complex as you want it to be. It can be very, very easy if your approach to investing is straightforward. It ultimately depends on how you want to invest. For example, do you want to invest in individual companies or in a collection of companies? Each of these approaches requires different levels of interest and attention as a first-time investor. I always encourage people to start with the simple approach.

As a first-time investor, you don't want to feel overwhelmed, particularly if you have a busy family life, a career or a business that you're running. The last thing you want to do is spend time in front of a computer screen monitoring your investments every week or every month, so keeping things simple is paramount. The next chapter will cover many of the principles you need to know to help you keep things simple.

CHAPTER 12

WHY WE INVEST

To invest wisely, we must understand why we invest, why we should invest, and why investing has been a tremendous wealth-creation vehicle for generations.

My aim here is to give you a straight-talking, no BS, truthful appraisal of why investing has to be part of your plan if you want to become your own financial hero. In understanding why we need to invest, we can better understand how it works. We will be able to set our stall out right and manage our expectations of what investing can deliver and how it can improve our financial outlook with time.

> **'Inflation is as violent as a mugger, as frightening as an armed robber and as deadly as a hitman.'**
> **Ronald Reagan**

The first reason we must invest is inflation. We covered this earlier under the 'save early' part of my formula, but here is where we can delve a little deeper into the details of inflation.

WHAT INFLATION MEANS?

Inflation is the increase in the cost of goods and services around us. In other words, inflation is how we measure things becoming more expensive over time. When we talk about inflation, you will often hear the phrase 'in real terms' being used. For example, you're losing money 'in real terms', but what does that mean?

If you have £10 in your bank account, the £10 is still £10. However, with inflation, your £10 will turn into £9.80 over time, but you can still see £10 in your account. In real terms, in the real world, your £10 won't be able to purchase the same things you could have purchased when you first put it into your account. So in real terms, your £10 isn't keeping up with the cost of things increasing around you.

A very simple way to contextualise this in your daily life is to take note of any increases you experience when you do your weekly shop. If that goes from costing £50 a week to £55 a week, the increase that you're seeing is inflation. Inflation, quite simply, is the monster that eats away at your money.

Ten pounds from fifty years ago is worth £155.94 today due to inflation.

Let's go through an example to illustrate this a little bit further. If you paid £10 into your account fifty years ago and did nothing with it, you would need to have £155.94 today to purchase the same thing that £10 would have bought back then. That means, over fifty years, the price of things has risen so much that your £10 is now just about worthless. In this example, the average inflation rate is 5.15 per cent per year. It also means that the price of things will be 15.59 times higher on average than fifty years ago.

When you take a step back from those numbers, you start to realise that if you want your money to be worth something ten, twenty or thirty years from now, it is crucial that you make your money work as hard as possible to outpace the prevailing inflation rate (the rate by which things become more expensive in society). If I had to put a number on it, based on the example above, you need to ensure your money works at a rate that generates a return over and above 5.15 per cent yearly. That's how much your money would need to grow by every year for £10 to be worth £155.94 fifty years later. This is why we invest, because throughout history there has been no other place to allocate your money that would be able to generate such returns to grow your money for future use.

So, where does this leave us? A good place to start is to look at the target inflation rate set by central banks. This target has been 2 per cent for a considerable time. In other words, central banks such as the Bank of England and the Federal Reserve in the US have set their target for inflation at 2 per cent.

With this target, they are saying that 2 per cent is an acceptable rate by which the cost of goods and services can increase year on year without inflicting long-lasting financial pressure or damage to households and businesses. When you take 2 per cent as the target set by the Bank of England, that, in turn, becomes a minimum basic measure of the returns you would need from an investment to keep up with inflation. Any returns that you achieve over 2 per cent are returns that grow your money and help you create wealth and financial freedom into the future, provided that the 2 per cent target is not exceeded.

As a hypothetical theory, this is solid reasoning; however, in 2022, inflation was in the double digits, and central banks worldwide scrambled to bring it down to the target levels. This complicates the problem slightly but focuses even more on why investing is the primary way of combating inflation in the real world. The problem is, investing isn't without its challenges.

We briefly discussed stock markets and what stock markets are: markets where you can buy stock or shares in companies. There are many stock markets worldwide. You will find a long list of companies you can invest in on these markets. These companies will range from large multinational companies worth trillions of pounds, such as Apple, to companies worth a few hundred million. To track how these companies perform, they are often categorised into groups and tracked using something called an index. The S&P 500 is one such index that is spoken about a lot in the investment sphere because it tracks the performance of the top 500 companies globally.

The S&P 500 includes companies like Apple, Amazon, Microsoft, Alphabet (Google), Coca-Cola, Pepsi, Meta, Tesla, Disney and many more. These companies have strong foundations and financials. Some have been around for a very long time, and they are all extremely profitable businesses.

Besides the S&P 500, you also have the FTSE 100, an index that tracks the performance of the top 100 companies in the UK. There is a long list of these indices that you can invest in, in the modern age. The S&P 500, for example, has, throughout its existence, returned an average of about 10 per cent per year for the last century.

Going back to the equation of inflation, if the target rate of inflation set by the central bank is 2 per cent and you have invested in the S&P 500 with an average return of 10 per cent per year, you will quickly be able to see how investing is an important vehicle to grow your money and create wealth. In this instance, not only are you keeping up with the 2 per cent rate of inflation set by central banks, but you're also multiplying your money's value against that target inflation rate.

Let's bring this into context in the example I gave earlier of £10 from fifty years ago today being worth £155.94. In that example, the annual rate of inflation was 5.15 per cent. If an investment in the S&P 500 had returned 10 per cent a year, you would have kept up with the inflation rate and grown your money by a considerable margin for future use.

This brings us to the second reason we invest: wealth creation. Social media has done a phenomenal job convincing people that wealth is all about ostentatious displays. You've come across it a million times before; the pictures with the Lamborghini or Ferrari, the Rolex, the Audemars Piguet, the images of luxury holidays, high fashion, expensive restaurants and other grandiose posturing. The truth is wealth has nothing to do with such things. One of the saddest things I've observed on social media, particularly in finance, is how influencers have used these ostentatious displays of wealth to draw a generation of young people into scams and supposed investment schemes. These schemes end up being the money-makers for the influencer; ironically, that's how they generate their wealth, which has nothing to do with investing. It's a sad state of affairs when you observe this repeatedly happening across different sectors of the financial space, from crypto, forex, day trading and so on.

Ironically, the influencers who are the loudest with these grandiose displays are often in debt. They rent the supposed accoutrements of wealth because they know they are an attention grabber on social media. They are more concerned with looking like they have wealth than truly having it. There are a couple of definitions of wealth that I want to discuss to drive this point home. Here's the first definition.

Wealth is the abundance of valuable financial assets and physical possessions?

Financial assets are typically regarded as stocks, bonds or other investments. Physical possessions could be property, valuable pieces of art and/or jewellery. Wealth could be equated with the possession of luxury watches such as a Rolex, an Audemars Piguet or a Patek Philippe that are known for appreciation over time. It could also be the possession of physical gold bullion or other precious metals.

In the above definition of wealth, the operative word is 'valuable'. It refers to assets that appreciate over time. Most people who drive luxury cars are not driving around in an appreciating asset. Of course, there are exceptions, such as certain hypercars that are manufactured at lower numbers, or vintage cars.

Most cars lose value the minute they are driven off the showroom forecourt. They are bad investments and an even poorer barometer for measuring someone's wealth. If you're reading this, it's important that you start to question and look beyond the physical appearance of wealth. Your interpretation of what you think wealth is inevitably dictates your mindset and, therefore, the behaviours you exhibit. This will influence the habits that will either positively or negatively impact on your ability to become your own financial hero and start to build wealth of your own. The second definition of wealth is a simple one. It's an equation.

Your wealth is the total sum of your assets minus your liabilities

This is also referred to as your net worth and makes wealth more tangible and relevant in the real world. For example, if the total sum of the assets you own is £200,000 and the total liabilities you owe are £100,000, then your net worth or wealth is £100,000. This is a great and simple way to track your net worth and set yourself targets to grow it, year on year, by acquiring valuable financial assets and physical possessions. That's really what wealth creation is all about: the smart allocation of your money into investments and financial assets that will meet your financial needs in the future. Your financial needs may be early retirement. It may be buying your first home or sending your kids to university. It could be anything.

If there is one thing that you take away from this section of the book, I'd love it to be the realisation that you determine wealth and what it means to you. It shouldn't be dictated to you by anyone else. If you determine that the goal you want to aim for is a net worth of a billion pounds, go for it. If your definition of wealth is a net worth of £500,000, go for it. You get to decide. You should go back to part 3 of Task 1 and reflect again on your timeline and the goals you set there, because this will give you purpose. It will give you something to aim for when we start talking about how you invest and how to allocate your money later on in this chapter.

The third reason we invest is for compound interest. Albert Einstein said this about compound interest:

> **'Compound interest is the eighth wonder of the world. He who understands it, earns it. He who doesn't, pays it.'**

WHAT IS COMPOUND INTEREST?

Compound interest is when you get interest on the interest you earn. Let's use an example here: say you invest £100 into the stock market and, after the first year, your £100 has grown to £110. That's a 10 per cent return. In the second year of your investment, you will start to earn interest on the £110 you have in your investment account, not the £100 you originally invested.

This means you get a snowballing effect where you earn interest on interest. Over several years, your original investment would be worth far more than if you only received growth on your initial £100.

Below is a further illustration of the power of compound interest, assuming you invested £100 every single month for twenty years and managed a yearly return of 10 per cent (the same as the S&P 500 historically). Of course, past performance is no indication of future performance, and this outcome is not guaranteed.

Total deposits into investment – £24,000
Total interest or investment return – £51,936.88
Future investment value – £75.936.88

This outcome would look very different if you only received simple interest on the original amount invested. Here's what the above example would look like.

Total deposits into investment – £24,000
Total interest or investment return – £23,900
Future investment value – £47,900

The difference between simple interest and compound interest is quite staggering. Compound interest adds £28,068.88 in additional returns to your investment, and that number gets exponentially bigger the more you invest and the longer you invest for.

As you read this book, I want to challenge you to sit down and think about how you're using your money and ask what you can do better. At the beginning of this formula, we spoke about budgeting. We spoke about your essentials, non-essentials and 'other' pot. We have spoken about avoiding debt because debt is a drain on your future income and limits the scope and range of things you can deploy money into. We also spoke about saving early so that you have an emergency fund to give you a stable footing from which you can build and invest. With a healthy emergency fund behind you, you should be able to afford to invest without needing to access the money you're investing due to something unexpected happening. Thus far, the formula has intentionally got you to this juncture. If you follow the principles outlined in Parts B, A and S of this book, you will have laid the necessary foundations to make investing early work for you.

Regardless of what you can afford to invest every month, I would encourage you to look at the impact compound interest can have on the money you allocate into your 'other' pot to invest. Then go back to your timeline and think about how this part of the formula helps you achieve your goals. Compound interest is the most powerful tool at your disposal, but if you want to become your own financial hero, it's also worthwhile getting familiar with a little-known concept called the 'Rule of 72'.

THE RULE OF 72

The Rule of 72 is a rule-of-thumb calculation to determine how quickly your money will double when you invest. Let's run through a quick example. We've already spoken about the S&P 500 and how this has typically returned about 10 per cent per year for the last decade. Using the Rule of 72, we would take the return of the S&P 500, 10 per cent, and use it to divide 72. What you end up with is 7.2. This tells us that any money you invest in the S&P 500, assuming a return of 10 per cent per year, would take 7.2 years from now for your money to double. Naturally, the higher the rate of return you enter, the quicker your money is likely to double. Let's say you are looking at a return or an interest rate of 12 per cent; use it to divide 72, meaning your money will double in as little as six years. The Rule of 72 isn't going to magically predict the future for you, but it is a great way to look at investing and give yourself targets or a marker in the sand. It can act as a measurement to track your investment performance and the progress you make towards your goals.

The Rule of 72 can also help you make strategic financial decisions. For example, if inflation goes up from 2 per cent to 10 per cent, your money will lose half its value in 7.2 years. Knowing this can help you make better, more informed decisions about the cash you have lying around or be the decisive factor in your decision-making process. In today's world, where 1 per cent increases are casually dismissed, the Rule of 72 is a great way to calculate the impact of a 1 per cent increase or decrease in investment returns or inflation. However, it is worth noting that the Rule of 72 should not be used as a one-size-fits-all tool. Everyone has their unique set of circumstances that needs to be considered, and if you haven't taken onboard the other parts of my formula you're not going to be able to apply and use the rule to its full potential.

Key Points to Remember and Action

We must understand why we invest, why we should invest and why investing has been a tremendous wealth-creation vehicle for generations.

1. The first reason we must invest is inflation. Inflation is the silent monster that eats away at your money.

2. Compound interest is interest earned on interest. Albert Einstein called it the eighth wonder of the world. Regardless of what you can afford to invest every month, I would encourage you to look at the impact compound interest can have on the money you allocate into your 'other' pot to invest.

3. The Rule of 72 is a rule-of-thumb calculation to determine how quickly your money will double when you invest.

4. Investing has served as a source of wealth creation for generations; the S&P 500 is a great example of a group of companies that have delivered great results for investors in the past.

CHAPTER 13

INVESTOR PSYCHOLOGY

I remember the first time I invested money in the market. I had mixed emotions. The first thing I felt was excitement because, for years, I had watched people invest money and I acutely remember how satisfied they felt when their money worked for them. I also recall conversations I overheard between people concerning how secure they felt about the future because they had money invested that they knew was working hard for them, creating a sense of financial security.

I also felt nervous and a little fearful, which is normal for first-time investors and investors generally. Fear of loss is the main reason why some people don't invest. The prospect of losing their hard-earned money is horrendous and hard to get past. At the time, I was still unaware of how the markets worked. There were blind spots and holes in my knowledge. I had only a little bit of information, but enough to make a decision on how I wanted to get started.

'The investor's chief problem and worst enemy is himself.'
Benjamin Graham

The first time you invest you may feel trepidation; it's normal, especially when you're doing something new. You can find yourself obsessing about the small details and your understanding of them, constantly wondering if you've missed something. Should I research this aspect more or have I fully understood it? If there's one thing I've learnt during my career, it's that you don't know what you don't know until you know that you don't know it. This can lead to analysis paralysis and is generally unhelpful when venturing into something new. It would be best if you acknowledged that you can't get everything right 100 per cent of the time. We're human, we're fallible and prone to make mistakes; as such, we make the best decision based on the information we have and that's all we can do.

Benjamin Graham once said that the investor's chief problem and even his worst enemy is himself. Your emotions and ability to control them will be the most significant factor impacting on your investment journey. Your emotions will dictate your actions as the psychological battle between fear and greed ensues and influences your decision-making process. While it is posited that most human beings are rational, rationality rarely applies when it comes to finances, and it's fascinating. Financial matters are only sometimes resolved from a sensible, logical place. When we make financial decisions, there are more powerful forces at work than logic.

We all have an emotional attachment to money and if, like me, you didn't grow up around it, you could have a scarcity mindset, just as I did. The impact of that kind of mindset can be damaging in more than one way. I realised, for example, that not having money was a disadvantage to me, and that elicited a negative emotion. When I started making good money, I experienced a positive emotion, but I always felt nervous that it might all end abruptly, and that spilt over into my spending habits and ultimately my mindset when it came to investing. I was certain I was doing the right thing in investing and building for the future. However, my scarcity mindset was wreaking havoc in my head, telling me I could lose this money and if I did I wouldn't have the chance to enjoy it. In my first few years of investing, this would cause me to cash in my investments at the slightest hint of a downturn, which was counterproductive.

The sobering reality is that if you're investing in the markets and you don't cultivate the right mindset, it is doubtful you will cope well as an investor as markets go up and down. You need to be aware of the traits that will end up working against you as an investor.

1. RASHNESS

If you are the type of person who throws a tantrum when things aren't going your way, or you have a tendency to jump in to something without looking, this could impact adversely on you as an investor.

Rash, impulsive decision making when investing can lead to poor decisions and a propensity to see only part of a situation because you're focusing on the now. This often leads people to buy, sell and change positions based on their idea of what winning or losing is as it pertains to their investments. A yearly loss doesn't mean that your investment is at a loss. This is something I encountered as a financial adviser; clients would panic over a 2 per cent loss in a year but forget that they were up overall when taking into account the five-year performance of their investment. Rashness can lead to a very short-term view that doesn't serve you well in investing; you need to have a long-term outlook to be successful.

2. INVESTING FOR FUN

I hear this a lot, and while it is great to see people approaching investing with a fun attitude, fun should be a by-product of acquiring a skill or a result of success. Investing can be fun and should be, especially if you're investing in industries that you are interested in, but most investors I know take investing very seriously.

The issue with approaching investing as fun is that you will pay less attention to the details of what you're doing and where you're investing. I see this a lot with new investors dipping their toe in the water. They miss the important things and skip over the basics on the pretext that it's all a bit of fun. If you put money into things that you don't understand, you're gambling, not investing.

3. HERDING

This is something else I see a lot of in the investment space. It means doing what everybody else is doing, taking stock-picking advice, investment advice from someone who is investing in something because his mate is doing so. You lose your capacity to think rationally and critically when you herd. More worryingly, you're not thinking for yourself and are more likely to fall victim to confirmation bias in a bid to validate why you're following the herd.

Herding has characterised various scams across social media. Scammers successfully use it as social proof to legitimise the scam; after all, if your friends are doing it, their friends are doing it and you have family members who are doing it, how could it be a scam? You couple this with the promised monetary rewards, and all of a sudden you've bypassed your critical thinking and the scam seems plausible, especially as it also appeals to people's greed and laziness.

4. OVERCONFIDENCE

Overconfidence is the exaggerated belief that our abilities, rather than what's happening in the world, are responsible for the outcomes we've experienced.

This is rampant in investing. Suppose you invested in a company like Tesla in the ten years up to 2022. You will have seen your initial investment of £1,000 turn into £78,000. It would be very easy to attribute this return to your stock-picking skills and your knowledge of Tesla. Sure, mounting ecological concerns might have been a good reason to invest in an electric car maker, but the factors that led to the surge of the Tesla share price have nothing to do with your knowledge or the decision you made. Such things are outside your control, and are influenced by what happens within the business. You just so happened to buy in and the investment paid off. Ironically, when the return on investments is down, overconfidence is not something you see much of. Overconfidence only rears its head when investors make money on their investments.

This is very similar to self-attribution, where you credit positive, successful investment results to yourself but put all bad results down to external factors beyond your control. While this can be confidence boosting, what it develops is arrogance and an ignoring of the fact that we cannot influence the many factors that drive the market or the performance of businesses we invest in.

5. FOMO (FEAR OF MISSING OUT)

There is and will always be a shinier toy, a new stock, an unmissable opportunity, the chance of a lifetime to FOMO into. From the GameStop and AMC short squeeze of 2021 to the numerous crypto pump and dump schemes, FOMO is real. FOMO is irrationality by definition. It's the reason people make illogical, fundamentally unsound investments, fall victim to scams and become sceptical about investing when things inevitably go wrong. This coincides with the you-only-live-once

(YOLO) attitude that encourages risk taking. I largely agree with the need to take risks and seize the moment, but I've witnessed first hand that this frequently ends badly where an investment is involved.

In my experience, you can only truly develop a healthy investor's psychology when you have a clear goal that centres and dictates what you do and how you invest. This serves as a reference point during your investment journey to keep you on track. It will help you keep a level head, particularly when markets are down and your instinct is to run for the hills and protect yourself from further losses.

Key Points to Remember and Action

1. The sobering reality is that if you're investing in the markets and you don't cultivate the right mindset, it is doubtful that you will cope well as an investor as markets go up and down. You should be clear on your goal and the reason you're investing from the get-go.

2. Rash, impulsive decision making when investing can lead to poor decisions and a propensity to see only part of a situation because you're focusing on the now. Always think long term when you are investing.

3. Fun should be a by-product of acquiring a skill or a result of success. You should not be investing for fun.

4. Overconfidence only rears its head when investors make money on their investments. It's important to remain level-headed when investing.

5. FOMO is the reason people make illogical, fundamentally unsound investments. Investing because you're fearful of what you might miss out on is not a good enough reason to invest.

6. Investing because your friends and everyone you know is doing the same doesn't make something a good investment. Often, those opportunities end up being illegitimate.

CHAPTER 14

UNDERSTAND YOUR WHY

There are lots of reasons why people invest. Some want to do so for the future so that they can retire and enjoy the fruits of their labour. Others invest to fund university or private school fees for their children. Others again want to achieve balance by having some money invested to supplement an income so that they can work only three days a week.

I invest to ensure that I don't end up like my dad, who realised in his late fifties that he hadn't invested money into a pension and had no way of funding his retirement. What is *your* why? This is the most important question you need to answer before considering investing. Are you doing so because you have a genuine reason or because social media is telling you to? This question is important to ask, because your answer will serve as your North Star. It will be your guide and your centre point regarding how you invest, what you invest and the vehicles you use to do so.

When speaking at events, I often use a sat-nav analogy to explain this. Imagine you want to travel to a place you've never been before. You know the address and where it is, but you don't know the route there. Forty years ago, you would have pulled out a map and plotted the journey to your destination, but nowadays we have technology. Today, you simply enter the address of where you need to go, and the sat nav will take you there. All you have to do is follow the instructions. This analogy applies perfectly to the journey you will embark on when you invest. Your goal is the destination, how and what you are investing in is the vehicle that gets you there, but it's also important to remember that, as with many journeys, it won't always be a smooth ride.

You will have bumpy periods where your investments rise and fall. Circumstances may cause you to pause and restart. You will have a journey filled with emotions; sometimes, it will feel like an emotional rollercoaster. This comes with the territory. Unfortunately, in today's social media age, this side of investing isn't talked about enough and it's common for people to start investing with a very loose idea of their goals. Here are a couple of tips to help you set a goal that will serve you well.

1. BE SPECIFIC

The best goals are those that have specificity; it makes the goal tangible and measurable. You need specificity in what you want to achieve and in the actions you to take to accomplish the goal you will be setting. Too many people will note down their goal but not consider the practical steps they must take to get there. It takes effort and pragmatism to make it come to life. Let's look at a goal as an example of what this might look like.

Goal – university fees for daughter
Daughter's current age – three years old
Predicted university age – eighteen years old
Estimated university fees – £9,500 a year for four years
Estimated total fees – £38,000

Now that we have all the facts laid out we can begin to get specific with the steps we need to take to reach this goal. From the facts we have, we know we have a fifteen-year timeline to work with. We know that the monetary goal for university fees is £38,000, the equivalent to four years at university. In Task 1 on your timeline, you would place a marker at fifteen years with £38,000 as the target goal.

The next step is to assess how we tackle this based on our current income and financial situation. To do this, we need to know current income, outgoings and disposable income (if any). Let's assume the following:

Current monthly income – £3,500
Monthly expenditure – £2,000
Surplus monthly income – £1,000

In this example we have a good base to work with, as disposable income is available to allocate towards the goal. Our next consideration is finding out how much can be and needs to be sustainably allocated towards university fees. First, let's start with how much needs to be allocated.

15 years = 180 months
£38,000 divided by 180 = £211.11 (£212 rounded up)

The biggest benefit of specificity when working towards an objective is that it turns a large goal into much smaller achievable steps. Although £38,000 looks like a big number, when you break it down it's just a collection of smaller numbers that add up. Now that we know what amount needs to be allocated to the goal, the next question is how much can you afford to allocate. With a disposable income of £1,000 a month, £212 shouldn't be a problem, but you should still go back over your budget to account for the following.

First, consistency will be key to success; you don't want to over-promise and under-deliver, so you have to be pragmatic. You have to look beyond your present financial circumstances and think down the track about how and if your circumstances might change. Can you sustainably allocate £212 a month towards this goal? Could mortgage rates go up and increase your mortgage repayments? How likely is it you could see a reduction in your income? Could you envisage an increase in your income? Where might you expect an increase in your monthly expenditure? Will making a monthly investment commitment cause any financial pressure? What big purchases or financial outlays are coming down the track? Do you have an emergency fund? These are all very important questions.

If things don't stack up with your budget, you may need to move things around to accommodate them. This could mean some sacrifices, but it has to be sustainable. Too often, I coach people on structuring their finances after they've put in place a budget that restricts them. In almost every case, the adjustments they've made to their finances in order to work towards their goal are so painful that they want to give up. I encourage balance, finding the sweet spot between moving towards your goal and keeping yourself motivated and driven. For some people that means a meal out with friends once a month.

Once you have the answer to all of the questions above, the second thing to consider is how and where you will allocate this money. I always encourage automation where possible. A simple standing order or direct debit will save you having to remember to make the transfer, but to where?

In the above example, by saving £212 a month you would reach your goal. This might be the most suitable option for you. However, if you invested every month, the likelihood is that your investment will generate some returns throughout the fifteen-year time horizon, which you could use to reduce your monthly financial commitment.

Using a compound interest calculator, a regular monthly investment of £150 with an average return of 5 per cent a year for fifteen years will get you to £39,000. This won't account for any fees or charges you will pay along the way, but, as you can see, £150 a month is less of a commitment than £212 a month. Of course, your capital is at risk when investing, but it's evident that investment presents a compelling path towards your goal.

By being specific about what you want to achieve you are able to uncover the detail of the task before you. It will give you a clear sense of direction and highlight obstacles early on in the planning phase. It will help you create a clear roadmap that you can adjust and change to suit you and your circumstances, and give you a clear yardstick with which to measure your progress.

2. BE REALISTIC

Working towards a goal can give us purpose and a sense of fulfilment. Working towards something is what makes most of us tick, but it is easy to get carried away with ourselves, dreaming big but failing to call into question our capabilities. A goal isn't a goal if it's not rooted in reality; that's the difference between a goal and a dream. We must be realistic.

Sticking with the same example as above, reaching the goal would be unrealistic if the budget in question looked like this:

Current monthly income – £1,800
Monthly expenditure – £1,583
Surplus monthly income – £217

You might argue that this could still work because there is surplus income to allocate, but the real question is how sustainable would it be? I would argue there isn't sufficient headroom in the disposable income to execute a plan sustainably. If the cost of rent, mortgage, energy, food or fuel went up, the surplus income in this budget would be decimated. Knowing this early on can highlight the need to earn more money, gain a promotion, move roles, start a side hustle, or set in place any other measures that would help improve the chances of achieving the goal. This requires complete honesty and it can feel brutal admitting that you're not where you need to be, but it can also be motivating and empowering. It's all about perspective.

Key Points to Remember and Action

I invest to ensure that I don't end up like my dad, who realised in his late fifties that he hadn't invested money into a pension and had no way of funding his retirement. I don't want that to be me. What is your reason for investing?

1. Your goal is the destination, how and what you are investing in is the vehicle that gets you there, but it's also important to remember that, as with many journeys, it won't always be a smooth ride. Make sure you are fully aware of the investment risk before you begin investing. There is no such thing as a risk-free investment.

2. The best goals are those that have specificity; it makes the goal tangible and measurable. When setting out, be clear about what you want to achieve and the timescale you need in order to achieve it.

3. A goal isn't a goal if it's not rooted in reality; that's the difference between a goal and a dream. Don't cheat yourself or allow yourself to get carried away with the excitement of setting a goal.

4. Be realistic and think about how you can set your goals in motion sustainably. Consistent forward momentum is better than stopping and starting.

CHAPTER 15

UNDERSTANDING RISK

I must tell you honestly and directly, investing can be risky. Social media is doing a great job of perpetuating a narrative that is opposite to the reality. It will have you believe that investing is a quick win and an easy way to make money, that there is zero risk, that you're always guaranteed a return, that you can put your money in today and within a matter of days get a double-digit or triple-digit return.

This is false. There are no guaranteed returns in investing, and you will always be exposed to some capital risk. Although this is true, you mustn't let it be an excuse for not investing. In this part of the formula we are going to talk about risk and what it means. By the time we finish, you will have a greater understanding not just of what risk means but also of how you might manage it and square it off psychologically as you begin investing.

WHAT IS RISK?

When we talk about risk, what we are referring to is investment risk. According to the *Economic Times*, 'Investment Risk is the probability or likelihood of losses relative to the expected return of a particular investment.' That's quite a mouthful and might need a reread or two, but it makes the point. A more digestible way to define investment risk is to say that it is the uncertainty of returns from your investment or the possibility that your investment could fall in value.

We noted earlier how if you had invested £100 in Apple at the beginning of 2002, that £100 would have increased in value 130 times by mid-October 2019 as Apple grew. The share price of companies, however, changes every day, and it's perfectly plausible that you could buy shares in a company for £1 today, only for the share price of that company to be 80p tomorrow. In this instance, if you had bought 200 shares of this company at £1 a share, your investment of £200 will have fallen to £180. This is investment risk.

In reality, you rarely see the share prices of companies move to that extent on a day-to-day basis, but you need to recognise when you invest in a company that the share price will rise and fall over time. As investors we want our investments to end up positive in the long run and we are willing to take on an appropriate level of risk to achieve that. This leads us into the conversation of risk versus reward.

Remember, we invest because we believe that the companies we invest in will return profits in the future. If a company returns profits consistently, it will attract more investors, which, in turn, causes the share price of the company to increase. We believe that the products and services they render are integral to the lives we live and therefore will continue to remain in demand for years to come. Keeping with the Apple example, the iPhone revolutionised the smartphone sector and has been a steady stream of income for Apple since its launch in 2007. According to *Forbes*, in the ten years between 2007 and 2017, Apple sold 1.2 billion iPhones worth $738 billion. That's just the iPhone. The company has other products; for example, Apple AirPods generated $12 billion in revenue in 2020 – that's more than Spotify and Adobe could manage across their entire businesses. When you add in the iPad, MacBook, Apple Watch, Mac Pro and their software offerings you are looking at a well-diversified business with multiple products and services.

Risk versus reward is about considering the risk associated with an investment and comparing that with the potential upside you hope to achieve. What you invest in is a key factor in this consideration. In the case of Apple, you could argue that the risk versus the potential upside is relatively small. However, if the company in question is one that doesn't have a diverse suite of products or services and isn't generating a lot of money, the equation would tilt to the riskier side. The risk versus reward equation scrutinises the probability of Apple continuing to grow and being successful in the future versus Apple losing market share and failing as a business. When you're investing, you are considering all of these factors and trying to make an educated guess on what you think the outcome or the answer to those considerations will be.

As investors, we all have a loss aversion. This is the idea that investors can be so fearful of losses that they focus more on trying to avoid a loss than on making gains. This is a broad topic in behavioural finance and poses interesting questions about why and how we make financial decisions.

Over recent years, there have been some very public examples of how risk and risk management have been overlooked. Think back to the GameStop and AMC saga of 2021. Wallstreet Bets mobilised an army of retail investors (ordinary people) against the hedge funds on a risky investment. There were YouTube livestreams, Telegram groups, Discord groups and Reddit forums dedicated to showing market movements and how much money was to be made. This led to a euphoric frenzy of investors piling their life savings into trading positions with a view to making a fortune. That episode was life changing for some who participated. People were able to pay off their mortgages and student loans. Others, who knew what they were doing, even made millions. And that's just the stories that were publicised. However, the stories that were not told were of those who lost their life savings, who invested thinking that they were entering into a guaranteed money spinner and instead lost money. They didn't understand the risk and didn't quite appreciate how fast things can change.

In this instance, you could argue that many of those who took part didn't properly understand the associated risk. They saw more reward than risk. They were making emotive decisions without taking the time to understand what they were about to do. There was also added layers: everyone was doing this (herding), so should I join in to make sure I don't miss out

(FOMO)? This is the wrong way to approach investment decisions.

The reality is, for most people who want to invest, risk is always a careful consideration. As a financial adviser, there are a number of ways to measure how someone perceives risk. The following question is a great starting point in understanding how you think about it and how it impacts on your thought process and decision making.

Imagine you are given £800 to invest and have two options:

Option A: Invest £800 for a possible return of 50 per cent
Option B: Invest £800 for a guaranteed return of £400

Which did you choose?

When you look at the two options presented, they appear to have a similar outcome, but when this was put to a focus group, option B was more commonly selected. Why? Because option B has the certainty of a known return while option A only has a possible return.

For the focus group, option B presented the better outcome and balance in the risk vs reward equation. It also bypasses loss aversion because of the known outcome. This would indicate a low risk tolerance based on the options presented. If those in the focus group were more risk tolerant they might have considered option A, which has an array of possible outcomes. A possible return of 50 per cent suggests that the return could be more than 50 per cent but it could also be less. Option A also presents the possible outcome as a percentage, which can sometimes be unrelatable because it doesn't clearly present a monetary amount. It's debatable if the focus group would have chosen option A had the question read 'Invest £800 for a possible return of £400', but it would probably have been viewed differently had it read 'Invest £800 for a possible return of £600'. Let's test it.

Option A: Invest £800 for a possible return of £600
Option B: Invest £800 for a guaranteed return of £400

Which option did you choose now? Did it make you rethink your previous answer? If so, why? If not, why? Note your thoughts down.

Risk management is not about positioning yourself to make the most money during the time in which your investment is invested. It's a balancing act between your desired outcome and the risk that you are willing and able to take to achieve your desired outcome.

ATTITUDE TO RISK AND CAPACITY FOR LOSS

As a financial adviser, I would spend considerable time talking to clients about their attitude to risk and capacity for loss. These sound complex, but they're quite simple to understand and you need to grasp these two concepts. Let's start with attitude to risk.

Attitude to risk
Attitude to risk describes the risk you are willing to take to achieve your desired outcome.

Staying with the example we've been using thus far, take another look at the hypothetical scenario below.

Goal – university fees for daughter
Daughter's current age – three years old
Predicted university age – eighteen years old
Estimated university fees – £9,500 a year for four years
Estimated total fees – £38,000

Now put yourself in the position of the parent and ask yourself what level of risk you are willing to take to ensure you can cover the university fees for your daughter in fifteen years' time. Plot yourself on a risk scale of 1 to 10, 1 being no risk, 10 being high risk.

How did you score yourself? Are you a 3, an 8, maybe a 6? Most people I used to advise tended to put themselves higher on the scale than they actually were. They may have scored themselves 8/10 or 9/10, but when we went through an exercise to delve deeper into the risk they were able to take, they ended up much lower on the scale than they had initially thought they were.

Your attitude to risk is the initial salvo in trying to understand how you feel about risk, but crucially it isn't the main factor you need to take into consideration. There are practicalities that need to be considered and prepared for, and that's where capacity for loss comes in.

Capacity for loss

If I asked how much you could afford to lose in your investment before it started to impact on your day-to-day living, what would the answer be?

I used to ask clients this question and it would get them thinking. The uncomfortable fact about investing is that you could invest money and see the value of your investment drop by 5 or 10 per cent at any given time. You have no control over the factors that could cause such losses, but you can position your investments so that you don't sustain as much of a loss. With that in mind, you need to have certain things in place before you jump in at the deep end. The most important of these is an emergency fund, which we covered earlier in 'Save Early'.

An emergency fund will give you the confidence to invest in the markets knowing that you will still be able to pay your bills should you lose your job, be unable to work or find yourself long-term ill. Many people overlook this and find themselves between a rock and a hard place needing to access their investments when the markets are down. This is a bad place to be and something you want to avoid at all costs. You want to plan for the worst and hope for the best.

Your capacity for loss is about your financial resilience to absorb investment losses when they occur without needing to cash in your investment. A healthy emergency fund is integral to this, as is good control over your budget and debt.

Capacity for loss describes the risk you are able to take to achieve your desired outcome.

Because many people don't have an emergency fund or haven't yet built up a sufficiently large one, their attitude to risk (risk they are willing take) on a scale of 1 to 10 can go from a 7 to a 5 or a 9 to a 6. If you have a low capacity for loss, your attitude to risk (risk you are willing to take) will be reduced; conversely, if you have a high capacity for loss, your attitude to risk can be increased.

There are cases where your capacity for loss doesn't necessarily mean you have to reduce the risk you're willing to take (attitude to risk). That's what we are going to talk about next: your investment time horizon and timeline theory.

TIME HORIZON AND TIMELINE THEORY

The level of risk you can afford to take can also be determined by how far into the future your goal is and how long you're investing for. Let's revisit our prior example of working towards funding university fees.

Goal – university fees for daughter
Daughter's current age – three years old
Predicted university age – eighteen years old
Estimated university fees – £9,500 a year for four years
Estimated total fees – £38,000

The time to achieving the goal is fifteen years, which is a decade and a half, long enough to ride out any market volatility within an investment. A fifteen-year time horizon will mean that you can afford to take more risk than if your child was aged thirteen and university was five years away. Because you have less time on the clock with a five-year horizon, timeline theory suggests that you should take less risk in your investment. This is because you will not have sufficient time to ride out market volatility or a market crash. So, in other words, the longer you invest, the more risk you can afford to take, and the shorter time you invest, the less risk you can afford to take.

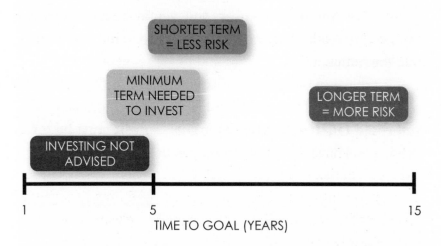

At the outset of your investment journey, you must acknowledge that markets are cyclical. What that means is that markets run in cycles; much like fashion where trends come back around, the markets have boom and bust periods. In the boom periods, you will make money on your investment, and in the bust periods, you will likely give back some of the gains you realised in the boom period. In the context of your time horizon, if you're investing for fifteen years you can afford to wait out any market falls and ride the recovery. If you're only investing for a short time, say five or six years, you may not have enough time for the markets to recover before you need to access the investment to meet your goal.

In 2007 and 2008 the stock market fell by nearly 50 per cent. It crashed and remained in a depression for eighteen months, taking six years to return to the previous high before the crash. If you had money invested in 2008 it would have taken until 2015 for you to make back any losses you would have sustained. If you had needed to take your money out within the six years it took the market to recover, you would have potentially cashed out at a loss or been forced to move your goal further into the future.

It is crucial to balance the risk you take with the goals you want to achieve. If you get the risk side of this equation wrong, you could fail at achieving your goal, so you must be level headed and have the ability to keep your eye on the ball.

Key Points to Remember and Action

There are no guaranteed returns in investing, and you will always be exposed to some capital risk.

1. Investment risk is the probability or likelihood of the occurrence of losses relative to the expected return of a particular investment.
2. A more digestible way to define investment risk is to say that it is the uncertainty of returns from your investment or the possibility that your investment could fall in value.
3. As investors we want our investments to end up in a positive position in the long run and we are willing to take on an appropriate level of risk to achieve that.

4. The share price of companies and therefore the value of your investments will change every day. This is normal.

5. Risk versus reward is about considering the risk associated with an investment and comparing that with the potential upside you hope to achieve.

6. Risk management is not about positioning yourself to make the most money during the time in which your investment is invested but reducing the propensity for you to lose money during that time.

7. Attitude to risk describes the risk you are willing to take to achieve your desired outcome.

8. Capacity for loss is the risk you are able to take to achieve your desired outcome.

9. The longer you invest for, the more risk you are able to take; conversely, the shorter time you're investing for, the less risk you can afford to take. This should always be considered in conjunction with your attitude to risk and capacity for loss.

CHAPTER 16

HOW INVESTMENTS WORK

Investing is when you begin to invest your money for profit. Investments have building blocks, known as asset classes, each of which have characteristics, including advantages and disadvantages. These building blocks can be used to manage the risk within an investment. An over- or under-utilisation of one or a combination of these building blocks can dial up or down your risk. Understanding your attitude to risk and your capacity for loss at the start of your investment journey will dictate how these building blocks are allocated in your investment.

In this chapter we will take an overview of the four most common asset classes: stocks, bonds, property and cash. All investments will have a combination of these four asset classes as part of their core composition. Having a basic understanding of what each of them is will help you when you begin investing later on.

STOCKS

Stocks are also referred to as equities or shares. The terms are used interchangeably, so it is important to understand that they refer to the same thing. A stock, share or equity is a company that is publicly traded on a stock market. The beauty of investing in these types of companies is that they are long-standing established businesses that are typically profitable and have a loyal customer base. They produce a product or render a service that is integral to our way of life, and as an investor in such a company you become a part owner (shareholder) because you own shares in that company. As a shareholder, you benefit when the share price increases or when the company decides to share its profits with shareholders. When a company does this, the payment is called a dividend, and many investors get excited about dividends because it's like a cherry on top of the cake.

It's worth noting that dividends can only be paid if a company is profitable, but that doesn't mean that all profitable businesses pay a dividend, and not all companies are profitable. An example of a profitable company that doesn't currently pay dividends is Tesla. Does that mean that Tesla is a bad investment? Not necessarily. It just means that instead of dispersing or sharing profits with shareholders, the company prefers to reinvest its profits into the business to grow. At the time of writing, there are many examples of companies that pay dividends, such as Coca-Cola, Verizon Media, AT&T, Johnson & Johnson and Unilever. There is an entire list of companies called the Dividend Aristocrats that have consistently paid dividends and increased their dividend pay-out to shareholders every year for the past twenty-five years. These publicly traded companies on the stock market will, in some way, shape or form, be part of your investment.

As exciting as this asset class sounds, it's important to note that it is the riskiest. It is where you are likely to make the most money from your investment, but it is also where you could potentially lose the most from your investment. This is because of market volatility and how the share prices of these companies will go up and down daily. From a risk point of view, it's important to understand how much of your money you want exposed to stocks in pursuit of your goals.

BONDS

The second asset class is bonds. I'm going to use an example to illustrate how bonds work, but broadly speaking, bonds are IOUs. They come in two forms: corporate bonds and government bonds.

Corporate bonds
Companies issue corporate bonds. Let's use an example. If Tesco wanted to finance a new superstore in Aberystwyth but didn't want to use its cash reserves, there are a few ways in which it could raise the money. A couple of things it might explore are taking a bank loan or raising capital using bonds. The interest rate a bank might charge on a loan may be more than Tesco is willing to pay, so it may decide to raise money using bonds instead. In this case, it goes to the general public,

asking: lend us £10,000, and we will give you back your capital after two years with a return each year of 3 per cent a year. This is a bond.

The rate of return (also called a coupon) on a bond will depend on the company in question. The rate offered will depend on several factors, but, typically, the higher the coupon, the bigger the risk and vice versa. All companies have credit scores just as people do; generally speaking, the better the credit score of the company, the more financially secure a company is deemed to be. As such, if a company has a great credit score it will offer a lower coupon because the risk of default is deemed minimal. The opposite applies to companies with poor credit scores.

These types of bonds will always carry a risk of default, but, generally speaking, that risk is deemed to be less than the market volatility you will experience in stocks or equities.

Government bonds

A government bond is the same as a corporate bond, only the body you lend money to is a government. An example is if the UK government needed to raise money for the National Health Service. It might ask people to lend it money, say £10,000, in return for which it might offer a coupon of 1.5 per cent a year. Typically, corporate bonds will yield a higher rate of return than a government bond. This is because a government like the UK's has never defaulted on its debts. It is therefore considered lower risk than a corporate bond.

With corporate bonds, it is worth noting that you are not buying shares in a company. As such, you are not a shareholder, and you won't benefit from any share price increase or dividend payments. The big advantage of a bond is that you have a known outcome from the get-go. The rate of return will be disclosed at the beginning and forms the bond's terms and conditions. The disadvantage with bonds is that the potential for returns is much lower than with other asset classes, such as equities, which we've already discussed. Bonds are considered to be in the low-risk spectrum.

PROPERTY

This is not residential property where you have private tenants paying rent. Rather, property in this context is commercial property. Commercial properties are used for commercial purposes. These will include toll roads, shopping malls, office blocks, warehouses and parking lots, to mention a few.

There are some clear advantages to commercial property. It typically attracts professional clientele and businesses with staffing and floor-space requirements that warrant high rentals and longer-term lease contracts. This gives you a good income stream and stability in your cash flow. You will probably see the value of that investment increase due to property appreciation as the years go by, with added value from the income it generates possibly adding a multiple.

The disadvantage with commercial property is that it isn't very liquid; something that you could sell quickly. Commercial property has run into problems in the past for not allowing customers to disinvest when the markets were volatile. You also have to be mindful of the impact of the wider property market on commercial property and the fact that there can be high costs to maintain and run commercial property. Still, this asset class is a medium-risk investment compared to the other two we have already covered.

CASH

The last asset class is cash. And yes, cash is vulnerable to the prevailing rate of inflation. If inflation is high, you potentially lose your purchasing power, which is why we invest. Still, typically within an investment portfolio, cash is held either to cover fees or as a buffer so that, when markets are volatile, it can be deployed to buy companies that may be falling in value but have good future potential. As you can imagine, this carries the lowest risk because it is cash. But the downside is that you have minimal opportunity for growth compared with equities and bonds.

As previously mentioned, how these four asset classes are used can either increase or decrease the level of risk within your investment. Here are some examples of how your investment might shape up, depending on your attitude to risk.

A low-risk investor might have 50 per cent in bonds, 30 per cent in equities/shares, 15 per cent in commercial property and 5 per cent in cash. A medium-risk investor might have 55 per cent in equities/shares, 20 per cent in bonds, 20 per cent in commercial property and 5 per cent in cash. Finally, a high-risk investor might have 70 per cent in equities/shares, 15 per cent in commercial property, 10 per cent in bonds and 5 per cent in cash.

With all investments the risk you are willing and able to take has a tangible impact on what returns you might achieve. The more risk you take, the greater the reward and the greater the risk of loss, and vice versa.

Key Points to Remember and Action

Investments have building blocks called asset classes and it's important you familiarise yourself with them and what they do in an investment.

1. All investments will have a combination of these four asset classes as part of their core composition. How your money is split across the four can be used to dial up or dial down the risk factor within your investment.

2. Stocks (equities or shares) are companies publicly traded on the stock market and are the riskiest of the asset classes.

3. Bonds are IOUs. You lend money to a government or a company (corporate) in exchange for a known rate of return from the outset. Corporate bonds can be riskier than government bonds but, generally speaking, bonds are deemed to be low risk.

4. Companies have credit scores just as people do; generally speaking, the better the credit score of the company, the lower the coupon on offer will be, and vice versa.

5. Government bonds are considered to be safer than corporate bonds, as it is unlikely that a government will default on repayment. As a result, the coupon on government bonds can be less attractive than that on a corporate bond.

6. Property in an investment is typically commercial property. Commercial properties can, among other things, be office blocks, shopping malls and toll roads. Commercial property is known for attracting a specific type of clientele. It can be expensive to maintain but can generate healthy income. It is deemed to be medium risk.

7. Cash is typically held either to cover fees or as a buffer so that, when markets are volatile, it can be deployed to buy companies that may be falling in value but have good future potential. Cash is deemed to be low risk, but it will be affected by inflation and has very little scope to grow. Most investments will hold only minimal amounts in cash.

CHAPTER 17

CHOOSING HOW TO START

If you've made it this far in the book and to this part of the formula, you may be excited or curious about how to begin investing. Whatever emotions you may be feeling right now, I encourage you to embrace them. If you're excited, you should be; investing is an essential step to creating future wealth and becoming your own financial hero. Wealthy people have used investing as a vehicle to sustain and grow their wealth for generations. If you're someone from a similar background to me where money was scarce, I hope this is the catalyst you need to start investing for the future.

If you're nervous, that's a good sign. It shows that you are interested and willing to dot the I's and cross the T's. You want to understand how you can safely put your best foot forward and avoid costly mistakes. In this section of the formula, we will go through two ways you can begin to start investing, considering specifically the DIY approach and the approach where you robo invest. This is what I wish someone had imparted to me when I started.

DIY INVESTING

DIY investing is when an individual or retail investor builds and manages their own investment portfolio. When I coach or speak at events, I use an analogy to position how this works, so let me introduce you to a box of Quality Street! I will be referencing it a lot in the analogy to help make sense of things.

As a DIY investor, there are several ways you can approach investing. You can stock pick, you can 'basket' invest, take a hybrid approach or robo invest. We will go through each of these, starting with stock picking.

Stock picking

Stock picking is when you choose the stocks (companies) you invest your money in yourself. Most individual stock pickers choose companies based on their interests or broader market research. As a DIY investor, there are endless stocks to pick from. Much like the box of Quality Street, you are trying to select your favourites from a range of companies. We've spoken a lot about Apple in this book, and as a DIY investor you may be looking for the best-established companies on the planet to invest in, but you might also be in the market for new start-ups that have the potential to be game changers and that are therefore a great investment for the future.

Deciding which companies to invest in and which not to can be quite an undertaking, particularly if you know nothing about the companies in question. If you've never come across a box of Quality Street before, you might not know what flavours are to your liking, and you'll probably try a few to see which ones you like and don't like. This is where stock picking can run the risk of being a trial-and-error exercise, and that's never a good way to start your investing journey. Picking your favourite from a box of Quality Street chocolates is much easier if you have prior experience; the same could be said for stock picking.

Coca-Cola and PepsiCo.
What makes one company a better
investment than the other?

Unlike picking chocolates out of a box, stock picking requires more attention and effort. There are crucial questions to be asked, and robust research is needed before you invest money into a company. You may come across similar businesses when you consider different companies as investments. For example, Coca-Cola and PepsiCo. What makes one company a better investment than the other? They both produce similar products and sell to the same customer segment. So, how would you differentiate between the two, and how would you allocate your money? Would you invest in one and not the other? If you invested in both, would you invest equally or favour one over the other? Would the amount of money you invest in each of them be based on revenue, dividend, market share or a combination of other factors? These are all legitimate questions that need to be asked and they can only be answered through research. Do you know what information you're looking for, where to look for that information and, more importantly, how to interpret it?

A company's financial accounts are a snapshot of the perform-ance and health of a business over a set period. Through the financial accounts, you can build a pretty good picture of what's happening in the business, where it might be facing challenges and where it is focusing its efforts for growth. The company's balance sheet can tell you if it has sufficient cash reserves to cover dividends and money it owes. All this information will feed into a much larger tapestry to help you decide if the company is a good investment, but do you know where to access a company's financial accounts and how to make sense of the information within them?

Most people underestimate the work that goes into stock picking and making those decisions independently. As a DIY investor, it's not just about the initial research. The onus is on you to manage your investment on an ongoing basis. The continuing management can be time-consuming and may not be something you can or want to commit to. This is particularly true if you have a busy family life or you're preoccupied with your career or running your business.

Social media is quick to reference the professionals, such as Peter Lynch and Warren Buffett for their investment returns, but they forget that Peter Lynch is not a one-man band. He will have a team of analysts working for and with him, looking for the best companies to invest in. They will have access to better information and to the Elon Musks and Tim Cooks of this world when making their decisions. As someone who has worked for several investment houses, I know that the daily market analysis produced is staggering. Be it from special stock market announcements that haven't hit the press yet, to buy and sell recommendations, professional investors have a clear advantage over the DIY investor.

In the past few years new start-ups are emerging, aiming to close the information gap for DIY investors. Some of them do the number crunching so you don't have to, but if you're serious about being a DIY investor and stock picking, nothing will serve you better than learning the ropes for real.

This will take time, but it could provide a knowledge base and skill set that will improve your life immeasurably.

'Basket' investing

The good news is that you don't have to be a stock picker to start investing. There are other ways of doing so that don't require in-depth research and ongoing investment management. Alongside Apple, other companies are equally, if not more, alluring for their own reasons. Coca-Cola, McDonald's, Amazon, Disney and Meta are just a few that come to mind. So, what if I told you that you can invest in all of those companies and more, simply through something called an index fund?

What's an index fund?

To understand what an index fund is, we first need to understand what an index is. An index is a way of measuring the performance of companies listed on a stock market. The S&P 500 (Standard & Poor's 500) is a stock market index that tracks the performance of the top 500 companies in the world. As such, you can buy the S&P 500 as an index fund. This means you can easily invest in all 500 companies in one simple way. Now, tell me that doesn't sound like a no-brainer.

Basket investing allows you to invest in more companies without the self-selection and the research that go along with it. Going back to the Quality Street analogy, if every chocolate was a company, you are not picking out your favourite. You're simply investing in every company. This allows you to pick more winners and fewer losers, and spread your investment risk across different companies and industries.

An exchange-traded fund or ETF is similar to an index fund. However, it is more flexible in how you use it. For example, with an index fund, you cannot sell your investment until the end of the trading day. With an ETF, you can sell your investment as long as the stock market and trading hours are open.

If you find stock picking overwhelming and want a far less intensive way to start investing, this could be a perfect option to explore. It's a method favoured by most because it's the easiest way to get started and doesn't require as much research. It takes away a lot of the thinking, saves time, is low cost and is less risky than stock picking.

The hybrid approach

There is another way to start investing that kills two birds with one stone. This approach will give you the ability to pick individual stocks and use index funds and ETFs. If you use this approach, you will still need to research the companies you choose. However, these companies will form a smaller proportion of your overall portfolio, reducing your overall risk. This approach is called a core–satellite approach, and here's an overview of how it works.

The core–satellite approach divides your investment portfolio into two parts: a core and a satellite. The core of your investment will consist of low-risk elements such as an index fund or ETF while the satellite portion of your investment will be made up of higher-risk stock picks of your own. The idea behind the core–satellite approach is that the core of the investment provides a stable foundation for the overall portfolio. In contrast, the satellite provides the opportunity to speculate for higher risk through individual stock picks. Here's how it might work in practice.

The key thing to remember about the core is that it will hold the majority of your money in the investment. In your core, you may have an index fund or an ETF invested in an index such as the S&P 500 or similar. On a percentage level, your core might hold 80 per cent of your investment, while the satellite carries the remaining 20 per cent. You can flex the percentage to your liking, but it would be counterproductive to flip it on its head and have 20 per cent in the core and 80 per cent in the satellite. That defeats the objective.

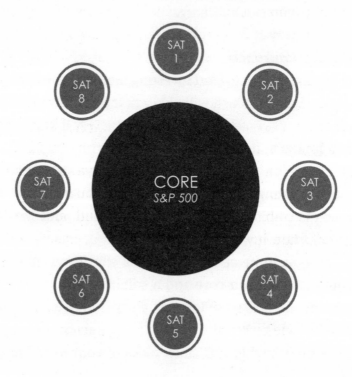

A potential benefit of using the core–satellite approach is that it can help you reduce the overall cost of investing. This is because the core portion of your investment is invested in index funds and ETFs, which tend to have lower fees. Keeping your cost low is important when you begin to invest for the first time because the fees you pay directly reduce the return you achieve.

So, what's available to you if you don't want to DIY invest? What if you don't have the time or don't want the responsibility of selecting stocks and ETFs on your own? Well, you're in luck because there is another way.

Robo investing

If you're the person I've just described, robo investing may be the solution you're looking for. It automates the investing process. This way of investing is relatively new but has proven popular worldwide because it has simplified what it means to invest while removing the traditional barriers for ordinary people. Many robo-investing apps and platforms have popped up over the last few years, and they all do away with the need to hire a financial adviser when you're starting out. Instead, they provide a low-cost, efficient, hands-off way to invest.

A robo-investing service will take you through a risk questionnaire to establish your attitude to risk and put you into a risk-appropriate investment that suits you, based on how long you want to invest. It will do all the heavy lifting by managing your investment on your behalf, which could work in your favour if you're the kind of person who would rather spend your time focusing on things you consider to be more important.

You may find robo investing offered in two forms: passive and active. The main difference between the two is the approach to managing your investment. A passive approach will track the performance of a particular market index such as the S&P 500. This means that if the S&P 500 rises, your investment will rise, but your investment will also fall if it falls. The passive approach involves no intentional or strategic intervention on your behalf. By contrast, an active approach will involve frequent human interventions by professionals managing your investment in an attempt to gain higher returns. In a rising market, this approach can be deemed unnecessary. However, in a falling market, there is likely to be some form of strategic intervention needed to stop you from losing the gains you made when markets were going up. Some investors like the latter approach because of the human interventions. Still, it is worth noting that an active approach will cost more than a passive approach because of the expertise being deployed.

If you choose robo investing as a chosen path, you will also lose your ability to choose the companies you invest in, meaning that you can't dictate what companies you want to be invested in. That said, it is quite possible that any company you have an interest in will already be included in your investment. This will almost certainly be the case if you are interested in an established company like Apple or Amazon. Such companies are included in 99.9 per cent of investment portfolios.

Another thing that frustrates people who robo invest is that most robo-investing services will use index funds and ETFs as the core components of their offering. This can be annoying, given that you could buy the same index funds and ETFs yourself and bypass the additional fees you will inevitably be charged by the provider or app creating an appropriate investment to suit you.

COSTS AND FEES

Fees are a fact of life and a fact of investing. They are important because they can have a significant impact on the returns of your investment. High fees can eat into your returns, while low fees can help you keep more of them. You must be aware of the cost and fees you're paying, but it's not the most significant consideration. When I worked in Canary Wharf we had a saying, 'Cost is only an issue in the absence of value,' meaning that if something provides a lot of value, then the cost of that thing isn't important. For example, if an investment carries a high fee but has a strong track record of generating high returns, the high fee may not be much of an issue because the value of the investment returns is greater than the cost of the fee.

This is particularly pertinent when trying to decide how you want to start investing.

The fees associated with investing can vary depending on the type of investment and how you invest. However, here are some of the common fees you might come across.

Management fees: Most investment platforms charge a management fee for the ongoing management of your investment. This fee is typically shown as a percentage and can range between 0.25 per cent and 0.5 per cent, or more. You can bypass this fee if you decide to DIY invest yourself. However, this approach has a time–cost implication, and it could also cost you in returns, especially if you're learning the ropes.

Trading fees: Some platforms charge a fee whenever you buy or sell shares in a company (trade). Trading fees are typically a flat fee or a percentage of the trade value. For example, if you bought ten shares of Apple in one transaction, that would be classed as one trade and would attract a single trading fee. If you bought one share in Apple in ten different transactions, that would be classed as ten trades, and you would pay the trading fee ten times.

Account fees: An account fee is a fee charged to an investor for holding an investment account. It's typically charged monthly or annually. Most platforms charge an account fee to cover the cost of setting up, maintaining, closing or transferring your account.

Ongoing fees: This is a fee some platforms charge for the ongoing management of your investment. Typically it's represented as a yearly cost and is a percentage of how much your investment is worth. It can range anywhere between 0.12 per cent and 1 per cent.

Fees can drain your investment, especially when you might be getting negative returns and your money isn't growing. In general, fees can vary depending on how you decide to invest.

Because the fees you pay will reduce your investment return, it's important to carefully review any associated fees before making a decision. You want to be sure you're getting the best value for money.

Key Points to Remember and Action

1. There are two ways you can begin investing. The first is DIY investing, meaning you make all the investment decisions and you're in charge of your journey. Here, you can be a stock picker, which has become sexy due to social media, but it is a high-risk strategy.

2. When you pick stocks, you need to know how to research the companies you are interested in, how to read company accounts and how to manage the risk of your portfolio.

3. You need to know how to eliminate errors from your decision-making process to ensure that you are not making mistakes that could have been avoided or foreseen.

4. If you don't want the hassle of doing the research and ongoing management, you can start investing by using index funds and ETFs. This will allow you to invest in a whole group of companies instead of a select few, which can be a less stressful and time-consuming way of investing.

5. Alternatively, you can invest using the hybrid (core–satellite) approach. The critical thing to remember here is that the core should hold most of the value of your investment. The individual companies around the periphery should hold a much smaller percentage.

6. If you don't want to be a DIY investor, you may consider robo investing. Most robo-investing services are easily accessible, running on apps across iPhone and Android devices.

7. A major downside with a robo investing is that this approach can cost you more in fees because all investment decisions are made on your behalf.

8. Fees are part and parcel of your investing, so you must understand what fees you're paying. More crucially, you need to ensure that you are happy with the service being provided. Fees will erode your returns, so it's advisable to try and keep your fees as low as possible.

INVESTMENT ACCOUNTS

Once you've chosen how to invest, you will have to decide what investment account to use. There are several types to choose from, each of which has pros and cons. To help make your decision-making process as easy as possible, I will give an overview of the main account types you're likely to come across. There is a lot more to know about these accounts so further research will be needed on your part.

'The first rule of financial planning is tax efficiency first.'

One of the first things you learn as a financial adviser is the first rule of financial planning, and that is: tax efficiency first. Being tax efficient will ensure that you can keep as much of your return as possible, with all of your available tax allowances accounted for in the process. As an investor, this is also one of the first rules you must remember when considering what investment account you should open.

Individual savings account (ISA)

We've covered ISAs previously when looking at the types of savings accounts at your disposal under the 'Save Early' part of my formula. ISAs are also an option to explore when investing.

An ISA should be the first place you start as an investor because you can invest up to £20,000 into it every single tax year (between 6 April and 5 April). Every penny you invest is completely free from tax. This means no tax on your investment returns and more money in your pocket for future use.

ISAs come in several different varieties. We will cover stocks and shares ISAs, lifetime ISAs and junior ISAs.

- **Stocks and shares ISA:** Whether you're a DIY stock picker, investing in index funds or ETFs, using a hybrid (core–satellite) approach or robo investing, this should be your starting point. Naturally, this carries more risk than a cash ISA (covered in 'Save Early') because your money is invested.
- **Lifetime ISA:** This ISA is available to individuals under the age of forty who are saving or investing money towards their retirement or purchasing their first home. The Lifetime ISA or LISA was launched in 2017 and came with the promise of a 25 per cent bonus from the government for every £1 paid in up to the account limit of £4,000 per tax year. It is worth noting that your £4,000

allowance for this account is inclusive of the overall £20,000 ISA allowance you get every tax year. For instance, if you saved £4,000 into a LISA within the tax year, your remaining allowance would be £16,000.

- **Junior ISA:** This ISA is for parents who want to save or invest for their children. You can save or invest £9,000 (at the time of this book) every tax year for your children's future. It is worth noting that your child will legally take control of the money in the account when they turn eighteen.

A couple of things to note:

- At the time of writing, income from an ISA is free from income tax, making it a good source of income for people in retirement who have amassed decent sums over the years.
- There are specific rules for contributing to your ISA during a tax year. You want to make sure you don't fall foul of the contribution rules. Be sure to seek guidance or reach out to me on my website and socials.

PENSIONS

A pension is an investment account from which you will fund your retirement. It's vital and one that many overlook until it's too late. Don't be that person, please! This is what my dad was worried about and failed to pay attention to. There are two main types.

Workplace pension

If you are an employee in a business in the UK, you will have a workplace pension that you should be paying into. If you're not, I strongly urge you to fix that. In 2012, the UK government made it compulsory for employers to pay into a workplace pension on behalf of their employees (the minimum as of the time of writing is 3 per cent of your annual salary). It did this to reduce people's reliance on the state for their pension provisions and put the onus on individuals for their retirement planning. When investing, you should find out what your workplace pension scheme offers you before investing in a personal pension. In some cases, if you invest in a separate personal pension, you could be saying goodbye to free money from your employer.

Personal pension/SIPP

Personal pensions/SIPPs are typically more expensive than a workplace pension but allow you to invest in a pension on your own volition. They can be more flexible than your workplace pension as they allow you to decide what you want to invest in and how you invest, depending on what type of investor you are and numerous other factors.

If you're self-employed, you, unfortunately, don't have a workplace pension, so the onus is on you to make your own provisions. A personal pension is a great place to start.

If you're a director and an employee of your own business, you can contribute to a pension as a business expense, reducing your corporation tax.

It is worth noting that SIPPs (self-invested personal pensions) can be much more sophisticated than personal pensions. As a result, they are often more expensive than the former and you might need to take professional advice to determine which one is best for you.

Some things to note about pensions

1. In the UK, you cannot access your pension until you reach the age of fifty-five. As such, if you're likely to need access to your money before then, a LISA might be more appropriate. With that being said, I don't believe that a LISA should be your main vehicle to save for retirement. There are some drawbacks and considerations to be mindful of, so seek professional advice.

2. The UK's state pension age is set to increase in the coming years. This, alongside the introduction of auto-enrolment in 2012, continues to fuel the narrative that the state pension won't be around for much longer. In its current form, how the state pension is funded is highly unsustainable. If you're not taking personal responsibility for your retirement sooner rather than later, you could end up like my dad. Don't let that be you, please!

3. Contributions into your pension currently benefit from tax relief. This means you get a tax top-up on all of your contributions. For example, if you're a basic rate taxpayer in the UK, for every £100 you contribute to a pension, the government will add another £25.

4. Pensions are subject to income tax when you start to take an income from them. However, under current legislation, at the time of writing, you can access 25 per cent of your pension as a lump sum at age fifty-five. This means, if you had £100,000 in your pension on your fifty-fifth birthday,

you could withdraw £25,000 completely tax-free to do with as you please. No questions asked.

GENERAL INVESTMENT ACCOUNT (GIA)

A general investment account – a normal account that holds your investments. These have become a popular place to start for new investors.

- A GIA doesn't have a tax-free allowance like an ISA.
- A GIA will be subject to income tax, capital gains tax and dividends on all investments it holds in the UK. However, there are certain tax allowances available to help you keep more of your returns.
- GIAs will generally grant you instant access to your funds should you need them in a rush. The same does not apply to pensions, where under current legislation you can't access your money until you're fifty-five.
- A GIA has no maximum annual limits for contributions, unlike an ISA.

CHAPTER 18

MISTAKES TO AVOID

We've covered a lot in this part of the formula, and it would be remiss of me to close it without giving a few words of wisdom on mistakes to avoid when you start investing. At the outset of your journey, I want you to remember that nothing and no one is ever perfect. You will make mistakes, and you will look at the situation you find yourself in and recognise that there are lessons to be learnt. The important thing is to take those lessons forward, implement better practices and educate yourself on why that mistake happened so you can do better the next time around.

MISTAKE ONE: NOT INVESTING AT ALL

This one is obvious, given everything we've spoken about thus far in this book, but so many people who could be investing are not doing so. Failure to invest could be down to a lack of confidence, a lack of know-how, or any number of the myths we covered early on in this part of the formula. By not investing, we are cheating ourselves from taking advantage of the most powerful tools we have at our disposal: time and money. I remember my dad panicking when I was sixteen that he hadn't invested in a pension. I didn't understand what a pension was until I started working in Canary Wharf.

My dad was a very educated man. He spent years studying and getting degrees – a master's and a couple of PhDs – because he had a thirst for knowledge and always wanted to learn new things. In the midst of all this, he did what most of us are guilty of. He got caught up in the day-to-day of living and working and forgot to invest in a pension. Ultimately, he ran out of the one commodity that all of us have a finite supply of: time. When I look back, despite all the degrees my dad managed to acquire, he didn't understand money or investing, which meant he had to keep working until he suddenly died.

The truth is, there is no excuse not to start investing if you have enough income to do so, be that in a pension, an ISA or a general investment account. Time is your biggest asset; the sooner you get started, the more freedom and choice you'll be able to create for your future.

MISTAKE TWO: NOT FULLY UNDERSTANDING WHAT YOU ARE INVESTING IN

As the great Warren Buffett once said, never invest in a business you cannot understand. This is an easy trap to fall into as a new investor, especially given the hyperbole surrounding investing on social media. Such hyperbole can lure you into a false sense of security. It perpetuates the lie that all things go up and can cause you to put money into something that isn't suitable for achieving your goals.

Having a good understanding of what you're invested in can help you make sense of why your investments are down. It helps you to calmly evaluate the situation and make an educated decision on what your next move should or shouldn't be. If you don't understand what you're investing in you may not fully realise the potential risk and rewards associated with it. This can add more stress to what can already be a stressful endeavour, especially when you are seeing your investment value fall.

MISTAKE THREE: AVOID THINKING SHORT-TERM

If you're thinking about investing, you need to think long-term. For any investment, you need a minimum term of five years. If you're a month short, a day short of a five-year term, you should not be investing. The risk is too high because short-term investments are generally more susceptible to the ups and downs of the markets. This means that the value of any money invested can fall sharply and you may not have enough time to recover. Short-term investments also don't get the full benefit of compound interest, which is most impactful over longer terms.

MISTAKE FOUR: LACK OF PATIENCE

In my experience, those who lack patience are typically DIY investors who are picking individual stocks and find themselves glued to their phones or computer screen, constantly refreshing their investment values. This is natural, and even as an experienced investor it's easy to get fixated on your account value.

Psychological studies have shown that a lack of patience when investing can significantly hinder long-term investment success. One of the reasons for this is that a lack of patience can lead to impulsive decision making. I have seen this in hundreds of different instances where people buy one stock and then sell it because it hasn't gone up, only for the share price to go up once they've sold. It turns into a dog-chasing-its-own-tail cycle that never has a positive outcome because, of course, a dog can never catch its tail. When you lack patience, you get fixated on the short-term performance of your investment instead of its long-term potential. You must keep at the forefront of your mind the reason why you're investing in the first place. Refer back to your goals in part 3 of Task 1, revisit what you wrote down and remind yourself why the goal is important. Revisiting your goals from time to time will keep you grounded and help to combat any short-term impulses you might have.

MISTAKE FIVE: LETTING YOUR EMOTIONS GET THE BETTER OF YOU

This is not only a mistake to avoid, but equally a lesson to learn from. Believe me when I tell you that your investments will enter a phase when you will look at the balance and question why you invested. No matter how long I've been investing or how many people I know who've been doing the same, we all still look at our investment portfolio sometimes and question whether we've made the right decisions. This is down to the fact that, as human beings, we are driven by fear and greed. These are two powerful emotions that can have a major impact on your decision making. Fear can make you want to cash in your investment at the first sign of trouble, while greed can lead to reckless behaviour. Here's an example of how fear and greed can influence you.

In the last significant financial crash of 2007 and 2008, the markets fell by about 50 per cent. People who had their money invested in pension funds at the time would have seen considerable reductions in not only the investment value of their pension but also the income they could draw from their pensions to live on. In my time, I have met pensioners who thought it best to disinvest their pension to protect themselves from the downside, which on the surface seems pretty logical, but it's a decision taken due to fear.

What most pensioners (and investors alike) saw back then when they looked at their pension's value was a paper loss. A loss on paper only becomes real when you decide to sell, take your money and run. Some pensioners and other investors did just that in 2007 and 2008. They took a paper loss and made it real by selling the investment and cashing in their account balance. Had they remained invested during the six years it took the markets to recover and return to previous highs, their investment would have enjoyed all of the subsequent market growth.

MISTAKE SIX: TRYING TO TIME THE MARKET

Some of the most common questions I get asked are, Pete, when's the best time to invest? When should I start investing? When do you think the market is going to crash?

My response is the same every time – I don't know. Nobody knows, and those that claim to are grifters. There is no investment almanac that predicts future market crashes and entry points so that we can position ourselves to make a killing. It would be cool if we did, but we don't. As it is commonly understood, investing is about 'time in the market, not timing the market'. This has become a popular saying used to refer to the idea that, rather than trying to predict the short-term movements of the market, you are better off holding your investment for the long term. Over the long term, the stock market has consistently produced positive returns. By holding your investment for the long term, you're more likely to see better returns because you're participating in the market for longer, not trying to find the best moments to invest.

By trying to time the market, you will be cheating yourself of one of the most powerful concepts when it comes to investing – compound interest. The power of compounding lies in its ability to generate significant returns on your investment over time, but you have to be invested for this to work in your favour. While waiting for what you think is the perfect moment to invest, you're missing out on valuable investment time that you'll never get again. It is more beneficial to prioritise the time you can gain in the market over the perfect entry point.

MISTAKE SEVEN: NOT REVIEWING YOUR INVESTMENTS

This is a really important one, as I've already alluded to. Investing is a journey that will move you towards your goal over time. Even if your goal is five years away, there is a lot of time to elapse between now and then, and reviewing your investments regularly to ensure that you are on track to meet your goals is important.

Reviewing your goals once a year will do two things. First and foremost, it will give you a progress report on how you are doing. In this progress report, you'll look at the gains or losses you're making, giving you a juncture to decide to pivot or change things as you see fit. It will also teach you valuable things to help you make better decisions. By reviewing your investments every year, your chosen approach will either get validated or invalidated, and both outcomes are valuable. If your approach gets validated and you move positively towards your goal, you'll know you're on the right track. If, for some reason, your approach is invalidated, you will be able to adjust. Reviewing your investments will give you a psycho-logical boost that comes with the sense of accomplishment of getting closer to a goal.

When reviewing your investments, you're checking to see how they have performed over the previous twelve months, and you will be comparing that with where you expected to be at this stage of the journey. Some years you will be on track; in others, you may be behind for a host of reasons. If you are behind due to poor performance, it's key that you ask the right questions to ascertain if you need to change your approach. Has your chosen investment performed in line with other similar funds, or is it an outlier? How has the market as a whole performed? Are there any significant events that could have impacted on the performance of your investment? The answer to these questions will dictate what you do next. If you're a DIY investor, regular reviews like this are crucial to ensure that you don't miss something important. This is particularly vital if you are stock picking, as you will need to be more proactive in reviewing each of the companies you've chosen and perhaps do so more regularly than once a year. If you are robo investing, this will be done on your behalf, but it's still worth keeping abreast of how your investment has performed.

The other thing you should review yearly is the cost associ-ated with running your investments. It is common for investment fees to increase through the years regardless of how you're investing. A yearly review is a perfect opportunity to check those charges and ask why they've increased if they have. It could be the perfect time to change providers and shop for offers or improved services.

231

Reviewing your investments every single year also allows you to review your goals. Remember that things change, goals change, priorities change and people change.

If your goals have changed, you may need to tweak how you're investing. This is something that people often forget to do, and because circumstances can change so quickly within a short period, they find that their goals and how they are investing are no longer in alignment. When this happens, it's important to acknowledge it and to establish if you need a simple change or whether you need to re-evaluate your goals and set a new path forward.

Key Points to Remember and Action

1. The biggest mistake is not investing at all.
2. Psychological studies have shown that a lack of patience when investing can significantly hinder long-term investment success.
3. Investing is about 'time in the market, not timing the market'.
   - By holding your investments for the long term, you're more likely to see better returns because you're participating in the market for longer, not trying to find the best moments to invest.
   - Trying to time the market means you will be cheating yourself of one of the most powerful mechanisms when it comes to investing: compound interest.
4. The power of compounding lies in its ability to generate significant returns on your investments over time, but you have to be invested for this to work in your favour.

5. Another key mistake is not reviewing your investments.
   - Even if your goal is seven years away, there is a lot of time to elapse between now and then, and reviewing your investments regularly will help ensure that you stay on track to meet your goals.
   - When reviewing your investments, you're checking to see how they have performed over the previous twelve months, and you will be comparing that with where you expected to be at this stage of the journey. Always review your investing in full consideration of what's happened in the world around you.
6. When reviewing your investments, be sure to review your goals too.

PART 5

C: CREDIT SCORE

What if I told you that out there in the ether is a digital version of you? This digital version of you is a historic record of your financial decisions, behaviours and all the key financial choices you have ever made.

What if I told you that this digital persona is used to assess you for all future financial facilities you might apply for? The data that this digital persona carries will be the deciding factor as to whether or not you will be granted credit facilities to enable you to progress in your life, get on the property ladder and do the things that are most important to you.

It may sound a little Big Brother-ish, but that digital persona is real, and I only realised I had one because of my job in a bank. When I started to get on my feet, I began thinking about my aspirations. I had just got a promotion and with that came a car allowance. Naturally, I wanted a decent car, something comfortable for all the miles I would be doing, so I knew I had to apply for a car loan. Around the same time, I also turned my attention to getting on the property ladder. I knew this digital persona of mine held all of the financial mishaps and missteps I had made over the years, and that it could potentially stop me from getting on the property ladder in the future. I knew I had to do something about it.

Everyone has a digital persona, and it's called a credit score. We're not taught this in school; it flies under the radar, only to come to the surface when we're adults. It's there when we're making big financial decisions. It's the gatekeeper to acquiring assets and maybe even sometimes liabilities.

After years of working in financial services and my journey of being in debt, which I've been very open with you about, I have learnt a lot about correcting my credit score. When I was in debt, I'm sad to say that my credit score depicted someone who made poor financial decisions, had poor money management skills and could not be trusted with another person's money in a credit agreement. As such, my credit score was rock bottom, but through hard work and diligence with how I structured my finances, I've been able to go from a rock-bottom credit score to a top-tier high credit score.

Let's talk about your score, why it's so important, how it is measured, the credit reference agencies, your credit report and how to improve a bad credit score.

WHAT IS A CREDIT SCORE?

Your credit score is a digital record of your financial history translated into a mathematical score. Think of this as a report card for your finances. If you perform well, you get a good score. If you perform poorly, you'll have a bad score. For a long time, I had an abysmal score because of my history of debt and my inability to keep up with my monthly payments.

A credit score is created using a set of rules and information taken from your credit report. This information is aggregated and used to derive the score. Banks and lenders will use it to assess your creditworthiness for facilities such as mortgages, car finance, personal loans and credit cards.

According to research by TransUnion (one of the UK's three credit reference agencies), most people in the UK do not know how their credit score is used. The agency found that almost half of the people surveyed hadn't checked their credit scores for over a year. This resonates with me because before I understood what a credit score was and its impact on me, I never checked mine. At one point I didn't even know that it existed, and when I finally found out what it was, it made for such bad reading that I wouldn't subject myself to the indignity of looking at it. As you can probably tell, burying my head in the sand was a recurring theme in my financial life.

Your credit score updates monthly with new information gathered by the credit reference agencies (more on them later). This can increase and decrease your credit score from month to month. By keeping up to date with your credit score, you will quickly understand if anything negative has been added to your file and what you can do to change the information if it is incorrect.

'I'm glad my credit score deteriorated to the point where I couldn't get into any more debt.'

There are numerous myths about credit scores that I want to share and dispel. Some of these I believed, and I hope by sharing them that we can shed some light on them and bring things into perspective. Let's use this information to help you improve your credit standing, to help you put your best foot forward, because your credit score is the gateway to all manner of opportunities and possibilities.

MYTH ONE

The first myth I believed to be true was that there is a blacklist somewhere in the ether. That isn't true, and I can say this now, with hindsight, having learnt from mistakes that have cost me dearly. There are no blacklists with people's names on them. Credit reference agencies collect factual information and make this information available to lenders, who in turn use that information in conjunction with the personal information you provide to decide whether you're creditworthy or not. Each application is considered on its own merits, albeit your credit score does play a big part in the decision-making process.

MYTH TWO

The second myth I thought was true was that the credit agencies actually get to decide who receives credit, and, again, that is false. As just explained, the lenders and the banks ask the credit agencies for information about you. They then use that information, together with that which you provided in your application, to decide who gets accepted and who gets declined.

MYTH THREE

The third myth is that a declined application can damage your credit score. I thought this was true for many years, but here's what happens when you apply for credit. When you apply for a loan, the lenders will ask the credit reference agencies for information and use that information to decide if they accept your application. The lenders do not report back to the credit reference agency with their decision. However, the agency can surmise whether you got approved for the facility because, if approved, it will pop up on your credit report as a new facility. What damages your credit score is multiple searches within a short period. In other words, if you're looking for a loan or car finance, the last thing you should be doing is applying to four different lenders within a relatively short period. So, be pro-active, get some quotes to determine the best two or three rates on offer, and apply in order of preference.

MYTH FOUR

The fourth myth is that checking your credit score damages your score, which is false. Reviewing your credit score does not leave a record footprint. Checking it is important; I still check mine every month to make sure my score remains healthy. There are lots of free apps and services to help you access your credit score regularly.

MYTH FIVE

The fifth and last myth is that previous relationships will impact on your credit score. It is important to note that there is such a thing as a financial association. A financial association is created when you have a joint account, a joint credit facility or if you are acting as a guarantor for somebody. If you are a couple living together and have a joint bank account, this is a financial association. Suppose you have a joint credit card, a joint personal loan or a mortgage; these are all financial associations. A previous relationship could impact on you negatively if you separate and your financial associations are not severed. For example, if any missed or late payments occur from a financial association before they are severed, your credit score will take a hit.

CHAPTER 19

HOW CREDIT SCORES ARE MEASURED

Once I realised what a credit score was and that the persona I had created wasn't very flattering, it laid bare my bad decisions and my lack of financial acumen. I started to ask questions about what information was being collected, and how that information gets aggregated and translated into a score that painted me so badly.

To be honest, this is one of the mysteries of the modern financial system. Nobody really knows all of the sources of information that are being poured into creating your credit score and nobody really knows the formula that is used to score you. We do know that information comes from a number of sources, and once you understand what sort of sources these are you will start to be aware of the things you might be doing that could be damaging your score.

PAYMENT HISTORY

The first source of information that gets fed to the credit reference agencies and goes into your credit score is your payment history. This will include all your open credit facilities like loans, car finance, credit cards, store cards, mortgages and any others you may have. The information sent builds a picture of your payment history and whether you have any missed or late payments on record. This will help them establish if you have a good track record of paying back your debts.

Put yourself in the position of the lender. If someone came to you asking for a £10,000 loan you would want to know whether they have a solid track record of paying their debts on time. If there's a recurring theme of missed payments that cannot be explained away as a one-off occurrence or put down to an oversight, most lenders will decline any credit application.

It's worthwhile noting that all missed or late payments stay on your credit report for six years. That is a long time, but it gives the lenders the ability to look back over your payment history to ensure there are no patterns in your financial history that could be risky for them. If you have consistently missed payments, you can see how this can build a negative picture of you.

ELECTORAL ROLL

The electoral roll is used to ensure that only people who are eligible to vote can vote, but it is also used to assess credit applications and access someone's address history. From a lender's point of view, they are more likely to lend money to someone who has roots in a particular location over someone who changes address every six months. The electoral roll provides proof that you are or have been resident at an address and for how long. If you've lived in one place for a long time, it is more likely that you're settled, you hold down a job and you probably have family nearby. This demonstrates stability around your living arrangements and will give lenders the confidence that you're not going to abscond.

This aspect of my credit score worked against me for a long time because I was homeless, didn't have a forwarding address, and it wasn't possible to be registered at the homeless hostel. Even when I began to put down some roots, I didn't know that I needed to register on the electoral roll, so for a good number of years I lived at an address without registering that I lived there. I've since made sure to register at every address as soon as possible.

In order to register on the electoral roll, you have to be eligible to vote and there are some criteria to meet. In England and Wales, you need to be sixteen or older. In Scotland and Northern Ireland you have to be fourteen and seventeen years old respectively. In addition to meeting the age criteria, you must also be:

a British or Irish citizen;

a qualifying Commonwealth citizen who lives in the UK; or

an EU citizen residing in the UK.

If you're unable to get on the electoral roll because you do not meet these criteria, it's important that you keep other forms of proof of your address. Utility bills, for example, will suffice, but you can also add a note to your credit file with the credit reference agencies telling them why you are unable to add yourself to the electoral roll.

PERSONAL INFORMATION

Personal information like your age, occupation, employment status, income level and home ownership status is a large part of your digital persona with the credit reference agencies. It tells them more about you and where you are in life. For example, if you're aged eighteen applying for your first personal loan, your age could indicate that you're not necessarily in an established career just yet. Combining that information with your income – let's say you're earning £15,000 a year – may further reinforce the assumption that you're just starting out in the workplace. Contrast that with a high annual income of £40,000, which may suggest you're already in a stable career.

If you own your own home, it is very likely that you have equity in your property, which could indicate financial stability. Your income level also paints a picture that helps lenders gauge your affordability. For example, if you're applying for a loan of £25,000 but you're earning £10,000 a year, they will know very early that you won't meet their affordability criteria. However, a £25,000 loan application on a £60,000 a year income could well pass the affordability test. When you apply for a credit facility, the personal information the credit reference agency provides and the information you put on your application are critical in the credit assessment. This information will be double-checked for any inconsistencies or inaccuracies. If the information provided differs to that in your credit report it could raise a fraud alarm with the lenders.

COURT RECORDS

Court records are a pretty big source of information that lenders will be looking at when assessing you and your creditworthiness. Court records hold information about any county court judgments, individual voluntary arrangements, bankruptcies, debt relief orders and debt arrangement schemes. If you have been involved in any of these, you are going to see a significant reduction to your credit score. From a lender's point of view, any of the above arrangements earmarks you as a high-risk customer that they would not want to lend to. As such, if any of these show up on your credit file it is highly likely that you will be declined on any credit applications you make.

In recent years we have seen an explosion in the use of debt facilities. Interest rates have been very low, making it cheap to acquire debt, but we are now seeing an increase in default rates as people begin to struggle to keep up with their debt commitments and turn to individual voluntary arrangements and other ways to write off their debts. While these mechanisms can play a vital role in managing debt, it's important to realise that they remain on your credit report for six years and can significantly affect your future prospects. For example, if you declare bankruptcy, this can prevent you starting your business and being a director in your own company. It can even impact on your suitability for certain jobs across numerous industries.

I always encourage people to only look at individual voluntary arrangements, bankruptcies, debt relief orders and debt arrangement schemes as a means of last resort, and never before speaking to your lenders and asking for help.

YOUR CREDIT REPORT

I used to think that a credit report and credit score were the same thing. Like many people, I was completely unaware that they are different but intertwined at the same time. They are independent but work hand in hand. Your credit report is where all the information we just discussed is held, recorded and updated. Your report is ever evolving. It updates every thirty days and the reference agencies are constantly receiving streams of data from the various sources to help build an up-to-date picture of your digital persona. Your credit score is derived from the information in your credit report.

It is important that you keep up to date with your credit report each month, especially if you're in the process of applying for a meaningful credit facility such as a mortgage. I can't tell you the number of times, as a mortgage adviser, I've had a couple who have found the house they want to buy, they're excited about applying for the mortgage, but they get declined because there is something in their credit report. Had they checked their reports beforehand they would have been aware of any negative factors likely to lead to a decline and had sufficient time to fix them.

The good news is that there is no real excuse as to why you can't and shouldn't be checking your credit report on a monthly basis. There are lots of apps out there that will give you access to both your score and your report for free. Some of them will invite you to pay extra for additional tools and alerts, and they will advise you concerning factors that are working against you and give you tips on how you can improve and build up your credit score.

'You can access your credit report for free by applying for a one-off statutory credit report.'

If all else fails, you can access your credit report for free by applying for a one-off statutory credit report under the Consumer Credit Act 1974 and the General Data Protection Regulation. You can do this with any of the three credit reference agencies by submitting a statutory credit report request. This can be done online, and it's a relatively quick turnaround for you to get sight of your credit report.

THE CREDIT REFERENCE AGENCIES

In the UK there are three credit reference agencies: Experian, Equifax and TransUnion. When you apply for a credit facility, the lender that you've applied to will ask one or a combination of these three agencies for the data they have on you and this is what they use to assess your credit application.

Interestingly, it is possible for each of the credit reference agencies to hold different information about you, which is why it is advisable to check your credit report and monitor your credit score with all three agencies. This can be important for a number of reasons, but here's an example. We know that it's common for lenders to use one or any combination of the credit reference agencies to assess applications. If you apply for a loan after having recently been discharged from a bankruptcy, you'd want to make sure that the discharge note is on your file across all of the credit reference agencies. If one of the agencies didn't have the discharge on file and the lender happened to ask them to provide data on you, it's highly likely your application would get declined. So, from a practical point of view, it's really important to keep tabs on your credit score and your credit report with each of these agencies.

We've established that the credit reference agencies collect data that is contained, maintained and updated in your credit report. This data is then used to come up with a mathematical score called your credit score. All of the three credit reference agencies score in this way.

Equifax score out of 1,000

Experian score out of 999

TransUnion score out of 710

Suffice to say, the higher the score you achieve against their mark, the better the rates you are likely to be offered when applying for credit facilities. The poorer your score is, the more likely you are to be offered higher interest rates and possibly declined for credit facilities. To illustrate this a bit better, the Experian scoring card on page 250 illustrates what the scores mean for you.

Very poor is a score between 0 and 560. If you score here, you are more likely to be declined for any credit applications.

Poor is a score between 561 and 720. This is where you might be accepted for credit cards, loans and mortgages, but these will be offered at a higher interest rate, meaning you will pay more interest.

Fair is a score between 721 and 880. Here you're going to get okay interest rates, but you might not be offered a very high credit limit on something like a credit card.

Good is a score of 881 to 960. With this, you should get accepted for most credit applications you make but you might not get the very best deals on the market. The interest rate you get offered might not be the best, but it's better than for lower scores.

Excellent is a score between 961 to 999. This is Experian's top tier and you should get the best offers and best interest rates.

Your aim should be to get your score as high as possible with all the credit reference agencies.

	EXCELLENT 961–999	You should get the best credit cards, loans and mortgages (but there are no guarantees)
	GOOD 881–960	You should get most credit cards, loans and mortgages but you might not get the very best deals
	FAIR 721–880	You might get okay interest rates but your credit limits may not be very high
	POOR 561–720	You might be accepted for credit cards, loans and mortgages but they may have higher interest rates
	VERY POOR 0–560	You're more likely to be refused most credit cards, loans and mortgages

Experian scoring card.

Key Points to Remember and Action

Your credit score is a digital persona made up of data tracking your financial history.

1. Your payment history creates a picture of how good you are at keeping up with your debt repayments. The information being sent to the credit reference agencies is used to build a picture of your payment history and determine if you have any missed or late payments on record.
2. When you apply for a credit facility, the personal information the credit reference agency provides and the information you put on your application are critical in the credit assessment.
3. Your credit report and your credit score are not the same thing. Your credit score is derived from the information in your credit report.
4. It is important that you keep up to date with your credit report each month, especially if you're in the process of applying for a meaningful credit facility such as a mortgage. You can access your credit report for free by applying for a one-off statutory credit report under the Consumer Credit Act and the General Data Protection Regulation. You can do this with any of the three credit reference agencies by submitting a statutory credit report request.
5. There are three credit reference agencies: Experian, Equifax and TransUnion. When you apply for a credit facility, the lender that you've applied to will ask one or a combination of these three agencies for the data they have on you. It is possible for each of the credit reference agencies to hold different

information about you, which is why it is advisable to check your credit report and monitor your credit score with every one of these agencies on a monthly basis.

CHAPTER 20

HOW TO IMPROVE YOUR CREDIT SCORE

By now, I hope that you've learnt something new about your credit score and your credit report. When you completed part 3 of Task 1, you may have written down that your goal was to purchase your first home or to buy your dream car. Whatever your goal might be, a credit score will probably be an important part of the journey there. If you're like me and have struggled with debt and didn't have any financial education, you may be reading this and thinking that you need to take action. That's where I want you to be and where you need to be in order to improve your credit score. Here are some tips.

REGISTER ON THE ELECTORAL ROLL

We've covered the importance of this already. To register on the electoral roll, you have to be eligible to vote in the UK, but it's a simple matter of registering with your local council. If you are not eligible to vote in the UK, then some alternative proof of address, such as your utility bills or bank statements, will help provide a record of where you live. Registering on the electoral roll has been known to give credit scores a big boost as soon as it is passed on to credit reference agencies, so don't sleep on this one.

AVOID MISSED OR LATE PAYMENTS

Avoid missed or late payments. This one is a little obvious, but it makes perfect sense, given everything we've covered. If you are struggling financially, and making the minimum payment on your credit card is perhaps a stretch, this is where what we discussed in the budget element of this formula returns into play. Now would be the time to go back over your essential and your non-essential spending to see what you can cut. Make sure you speak to your creditors and explain that you are in difficulty. The last thing you should do is bury your head in the sand, hope for the best and never tackle the problem head-on. This will cause more damage than it's worth, so please ask for help from friends, family or any other support system you might have. If, as was the case with me, you don't have a support system, reach out to organisations like StepChange.

MONITOR YOUR CREDIT UTILISATION

The next thing you can do to improve your credit score is to keep a close eye on your credit utilisation rate. This is something I learnt the hard way. I'm going to use an example to illustrate this. If you have a credit card with a credit limit of £1,000 and your credit card is always maxed out at £1,000, it will be a negative factor on your credit score. It can indicate to lenders that you are under financial pressure and may struggle to repay the debt owed. This is particularly the case if you have a long, demonstrable track record of only making the minimum monthly payment. An ideal position is where you have headroom in your credit utilisation. Some credit reference agencies consider keeping your utilisation below 70 per cent of your credit limit to be an indication of a healthy financial balance. This means keeping credit utilisation on a credit card with a limit of £1,000 at £700 or below. It signals to the lender that you're not under any financial pressure.

PAY MORE THAN THE MINIMUM PAYMENT

This is important for signalling that you're not under financial pressure and don't lack basic budgeting skills. Making only the minimum payment, on the other hand, indicates that you're finding it difficult to pay down the debts you owe. We could, of course, be cynical and posit that the lenders want us to make just the minimum payments so as to keep their profits going, but that's also a risk to them in the long run. From a psychological point of view, paying the minimum amount can be soul destroying. I spent three years with a credit card balance that I only paid the minimum payment on, and every single time I looked at the statement, the number didn't budge. That impacted on my mental health because I felt anxious knowing I had this number hanging over my head. I had to go back over the basics we've covered in the budget part of this book to help me create a plan and move forward.

AVOID MULTIPLE APPLICATIONS

Again, this is a no-brainer and one you can easily avoid with preparation and forethought, but it is easy to fall victim to it in practice. I've done just that before. I applied for a credit card with three different providers within three days. For me, it painted a picture of desperation, of someone under financial pressure and needing to fill a gap, and that was exactly the case. I needed the credit card to cover a bill I hadn't accounted for. Multiple applications within a short period are a red flag to lenders.

In some cases, you may want to see if you will be pre-approved for a facility before you apply. More and more lenders are offering this by doing a soft search on your credit file. A soft search doesn't leave a footprint on your record and is the preferred way of checking your eligibility for a facility you are considering applying for. Hard searches leave a footprint on your record, so you want to be certain you will be approved before committing to one. It is common these days to have many facilities such as credit already pre-approved based on your credit score. If you monitor your credit score regularly, such offers may come to your attention. This can be a great way to avoid applying for facilities you cannot get. If you have a less than stellar credit score, it may mean that the interest rates you are offered are higher than others, but you can use any offers you receive to help you build and improve your score.

CHECK YOUR SCORE REGULARLY

By now, this should go without saying. Many apps will help you track your credit score and keep you up to date with your credit report for free. Most of them will send you notifications on what's changed, how to improve, and what is and isn't working in your favour. These are widely available services, and by keeping on top of your credit score you will have an advantage if you are planning for something big. For example, if in part 3 of Task 1 your goal is to purchase your first home, you will know ahead of time if you're in the best position to be accepted for a mortgage application, based on the information in your report. The same applies if you are looking to purchase a car or raise money for your business venture via a business loan. As mentioned earlier, I check my credit score every month. It takes me ten minutes to browse and see if anything significant has changed.

BONUS TIP

Occasionally, I have noticed things in my credit report that shouldn't have been there. For example, I once apparently missed a payment to a mobile phone provider. It should never have gone down as a missed payment. I had finished my contract, paid up in cash and cancelled the direct debit, but the network hadn't updated its systems in time before they applied for another direct debit payment. It went down in my credit report as a missed payment even though my contract was paid up. In this instance, I was able to challenge the missed payment in my report, and, below, I set out the six-step process involved in making such a challenge. Remember that there are three credit reference agencies in the UK – Experian, Equifax and TransUnion – so you will need to contact each one to ensure that the information they hold concerning you is uniform.

1. Contact the credit reference agencies and ask them to add a notice of the dispute to your file. This temporary marker highlights that a certain set of information is being investigated.

2. Within twenty-eight days, the reference agency has to investigate your enquiry with the relevant organisations and report its findings to you.

3. If the investigation finds that your credit report is inaccurate, the information in question will be corrected and/or removed. This was the outcome I achieved with my mobile phone provider all those years ago.

4. If, for whatever reason, the lender or provider insists that the information is correct, then the credit reference agency will remove the notice of dispute, and the information will remain on your file. That's when you go on to the next step.

5. If you still maintain that the information is incorrect and doesn't belong on your file, you can complain directly to the lender or provider and still add a notice of correction to your credit report, explaining what's happened and why you think the information doesn't belong on your file.

6. If you have raised your complaint with the lender and are dissatisfied with the outcome, you can refer the matter to the Financial Ombudsman Service or the Information Commissioner's Office. This will put a note on your file, which means that when you begin to apply for credit facilities, the lender you're applying to will have to consider the notice of correction when assessing your application. It doesn't mean you'll get accepted 100 per cent of the time, but it is a way to challenge incorrect information and have your say put on record.

Key Points to Remember and Action

1. Registering on the electoral roll has been known to give credit scores a big boost as soon as it is passed on to credit reference agencies.

2. Keep a close eye on your credit utilisation rate. If you have a credit card that is constantly maxed out, it can signal to lenders that you're under financial pressure and may not be able to keep up with your repayments. Some credit reference agencies consider keeping your utilisation below 70 per cent of your credit limit to be an indication of a healthy financial balance. This means keeping credit utilisation on a credit card with a limit of £1,000 at £700 or below.

3. Making only the minimum payment indicates that you're finding it difficult to pay down the debts you owe. Always try to pay more than the minimum payment on your credit cards.

4. It is common these days to have many facilities such as credit cards already pre-approved based on your credit score. When applying for credit, explore these options first, as you have a better chance of a successful application.

5. Many apps will help you track your credit score and keep you up to date with your credit report for free, but make sure you're monitoring your score with all three credit agencies.

AFTERWORD

We've covered a lot in this book, so if you've made it this far, I want to extend my deepest gratitude. I started on my journey to share the knowledge I gained in my career in 2020. The first YouTube video and podcast episode I ever posted went live on 7 and 19 January 2020, respectively. Two million YouTube views and 150 podcast episodes later, this book attempts to communicate some of the harsh yet uplifting lessons I've taken from my career and life thus far. My sincerest hope is that you've found at least one thing that has inspired you to take charge of your finances and change your life.

I created the B.A.S.I.C. formula to provide a ground-up view of some of the principles that have transformed my finances so spectacularly. As you move on, I want, finally, to give you some food for thought using a very brief exercise. All you have to do is continue with what you've been doing this whole time: read. Take a look at the words in all caps below:

OPPORTUNITYISNOWHERE

Recite back what you read. Read it again. Recite it back. Did you see it? Once more ... Once you finally see it, you can't un-see it. There you go. You got it!

See, there are two ways you could have read the words in all caps.

OPPORTUNITY IS NO WHERE

or

OPPORTUNITY IS NOW HERE

Life is about perspective and how we see the world around us. Parts of my formula may require you to make some uncomfortable choices. They may lead you to have uncomfortable conversations with yourself and others. If you've picked up this book, you're probably at a place where you know you need to equip yourself with the tools to succeed in your dealings with money. Well, the opportunity is now here to make that happen. The opportunity is now here to make changes and develop new habits that will pay a dividend for decades to come. I want to encourage you to be brave, bold, curious, and to ask questions. This is a journey, and, in the words of author and poet Jocelyn Soriano, 'Don't underestimate the power of small steps to build a great future.'

A USEFUL LIST OF PROVIDERS

My B.A.S.I.C. formula has taken you through the five key areas of your finances that you need to master to become your own financial hero. In this appendix, I list providers who offer products and services related to the various parts of the formula, except for one (Part 3 – Save Early). These companies predominantly provide services in the UK. If you are reading from within the Commonwealth or elsewhere, search for similar companies with similar offerings.

PART 1 – B: BUDGETING

Emma: The basic version of the Emma app is free and works like its peers by pooling your account data. But it focuses on categorising transactions and suggesting where you're overspending, including which of your bank accounts charges you the most in fees.

HyperJar: This budgeting app is designed to make it easier to plan, share and spend your money – and best of all, it's free to use. As its name implies, you can open different

'Jars' to allocate and organise your money for different purposes.

MoneyDashboard: This free budgeting app shows you all your finances in one dashboard, giving you an overview of your everyday spending via graphs and tables.

Moneyhub: This is a personalised service – as well as offering tech tools to help you budget, it gives you the option to speak with an adviser. You can also review accounts such as your mortgage, pensions and investments.

PART 2 – A: AVOID DEBT

Citizens Advice: Citizens Advice is one of the best resources for people in debt. Contrary to what most people think, Citizens Advice is not one charity but a collection of over three hundred charities across the UK.

Debt Advice Foundation: For those worried about tackling debts on their own, the Debt Advice Foundation offers support through setting up better financial arrangements with creditors for their personal circumstances. It offers free, impartial advice to people struggling with their outstanding balances and can recommend a debt solution scheme that suits their lifestyle.

National Debtline: This UK-wide telephone helpline specialises in offering both self-help for those in debt and assistance with establishing debt-management plans.

StepChange: This is a debt charity funded through the government, UK banks and other donations. It claims to offer the most comprehensive free debt advice process on the charitable market.

PART 4 – I: INVEST EARLY

DIY stock picking

eToro: With over a decade in the market, eToro enables you to buy and sell stocks and shares on the world's biggest stock exchanges. You buy stocks and cryptocurrencies here.

FinecoBank: FinecoBank (often shortened to just 'Fineco') is a popular choice for those who want to be exposed to global markets. It has a pretty detailed platform and lets you buy stock pick and a selection of index funds.

Freetrade: Freetrade is a free trading platform that's a popular choice for new investors looking for an attractive user interface and an easy-to-use platform. It will allow you to stock pick and buy Index Funds and ETFs.

Hargreaves Lansdown: The UK's biggest and most comprehensive wealth manager, this 'investment supermarket' is a popular choice for investors. It's a bit pricey, but it makes up for it with its mobile app and easy trades. You can stock pick here and buy a multitude of index funds.

Stake: Although founded in Australia, Stake has moved to the UK and allows you to trade US stocks and exchange-traded funds (ETFs). There are no brokerage fees, and you can stock pick and buy US ETFs.

Basket, hybrid and robo investing

InvestEngine: This is a relatively new investment platform that lets you choose between ready-made portfolios and a DIY option to choose a range of ETFs to invest in.

Moneyfarm: This investment app gives users access to general investment accounts (GIAs), ISAs and self-invested personal pensions (SIPPs). There are seven ready-to-go portfolios available, made up of ETFs. They are sorted according to your risk tolerance, so that you can choose the right option for your peace of mind. The Moneyfarm team actively manages investments to ensure you get value for money. There is even a dedicated consultant if you need somebody to discuss your investments with.

Wealthify: Wealthify offers plenty of investment opportunities. It is backed by one of the UK's largest financial services institutions – Aviva. Your money is invested according to your risk tolerance, in either a stocks and shares ISA, Junior ISA, GIA or pension.

PART 5 – C: CREDIT SCORE

ClearScore: This credit score app allows you to see your credit score whenever you log in and also to access your credit report. Alongside your score and credit report, it will also show you loans and credit cards you are likely to be accepted for based on your credit score. This means that you can apply with a greater degree of confidence.

Credit Karma: Credit Karma is the best-known service for getting free credit score reports from the Equifax and

TransUnion credit reference agencies. The Credit Karma app for Android and iOS provides alerts for any important changes to your credit report, and if you see any errors you can file a dispute from the app. The app also gives an organised summary of your credit score breakdown, including the accounts factored into your score.

Experian: They provide your score, updated every thirty days, in addition to details about credit card account activity, outstanding debt and the effects of your credit card activity on your score.

ABOUT THE AUTHOR

Peter Komolafe is a highly commended financial expert, financial coach and TV personality whose personal journey is the driving force behind his passion for helping ordinary people create financial security through positive financial habits.

Peter founded *Conversation of Money* (a YouTube channel and weekly podcast) in 2020 to have conversations he wished someone had had with him when he was in his twenties. Having struggled with debt through his twenties and thirties, his story has seen him go from foster care and being homeless to the executive team of a Fortune 100 company in Canary Wharf. Peter has been featured on *Lorraine*, *Steph's Packed Lunch*, BBC World Service, *The Times*, the *Express* and ITV, and he has appeared as the financial expert on *Secret Spenders: Beat the Price Rises* on Channel 4.

WEBSITE AND SOCIALS

Website – www.peterkomolafe.com
YouTube – www.youtube.com/@conversationofmoney
Instagram – www.instagram.com/conversationofmoney

ACKNOWLEDGEMENTS

I want to thank my partner Ilona Loewnau for always believing in me and continuing to be my rock.

Thanks too to my foster parents Sid and Sylvia Saunders, and my mum and my dad.

To Jack Freud, Michael Foster, Hattie Grunewald and the team at The Blair Partnership; also Rose Sandy and the team at HarperCollins for making this book possible, my copyeditor Nick Fawcett and my agent Julia Champion.

To Jenny Berry for giving me my first job in financial services and seeing something in me that I couldn't see myself.

To Mandy Mitchell for helping me make that first transition from retail banking to corporate banking and for being an awesome manager.

To Richard Horner and Jonathan Scannell for giving me the professional opportunities that changed my life.

To my close friends Nait 'JungleBoi' Masuku, Michael Antoine, Taka Inufusa and Lere Fagbulu for their sage advice. Thanks also to my colleagues and friends Terry Michael and Keith Jarrett for all the industry back-and-forth and support.

ACKNOWLEDGEMENTS

To EVERYONE who has followed me, watched me, liked, shared, commented, attended my YouTube Q&As and IG Lives, and listened to my podcast.

SOURCES

Chapter 2: The Essentials
Kiyosaki, Robert. *Rich Dad Poor Dad, 25th Anniversary edition*, Plata Publishing, 2022

Chapter 5: Making It Work for Real
Tayne, Leslie. https://www.amazon.co.uk/Life-Debt-Approach-Achieving-Financial-ebook/dp/B00SVKUP1A/ref=sr_1_1?crid=239P68G8YMUCV&keywords=Life+%26+Debt%3A+a+fresh+approach+to+achieving+financial+wellness&qid=1674489522&sprefix=life+%26+debt+a+fresh+approach+to+achieving+financial+wellness%2Caps%2C86&sr=8-1. *Life & Debt: A Fresh Approach to Achieving Financial Wellness*, Gateway Bridge Press, 2015

PART 2 – A: AVOID DEBT
Morris, Nathan. https://thewallet.today/quoteoftheday/Every-time-you-borrow-money-youre-robbing-your-future-self.-Nathan-W.Morris-20200722-0032.html

PART 3 – S: SAVE EARLY
Berkman, Elliot. hopesandfears.com
Money and Pensions Service. https://maps.org.uk
Denning, Tim. https://timdenning.medium.com
@TimDenning

Chapter 11: Saving Alone Isn't Enough
Bryant, Jane, *Making the Most of Your Money Now: The Classic Bestseller Completely Revised for the New Economy*, Simon & Schuster, 2009.

Chapter 20: How to Improve Your Credit Score
TransUnion. www.transunion.co.uk

INDEX